I Am

Other Titles in the
Teaching Sermon Series

THE TEACHING SERMON SERIES

Ronald J. Allen, Editor

I AM

Teaching Sermons on the Incarnation

PENELOPE DUCKWORTH

Abingdon Press
Nashville

I AM:
TEACHING SERMONS ON THE INCARNATION

Copyright © 1998 by Abingdon Press

This book is printed on elemental-chlorine-free paper.

Library of Congress Cataloging-in-Publication Data

Duckworth, Penelope, 1947–
    I am : teaching sermons on the Incarnation / Penelope Duckworth.
        p. cm.— (The teaching sermon series)
    Includes bibliographical references.
    ISBN 0-687-01359-3 (pbk. : alk. paper)
    1. Incarnation Sermons. 2. Teaching sermons. 3. Sermons, American. 4. Episcopal Church—Sermons. I. Title. II. Series.
BT220.D78   1998
232 '.1— dc21   98-20649
                                                                                                    CIP

A number of these sermons appeared previously in slightly different forms. Grateful acknowledgment is given to the following publications:

Best Sermons 3, edited by James W. Cox (San Francisco: Harper & Row, 1990), for "Disbelief for Joy" (which won First Place in the Doctrinal/Theological category).

Pulpit Digest, edited by David Albert Farmer, for " 'Who Touched Me?' " (May/June 1992), "Gifts and Revelations" (January/February 1995), " 'Yes, Lord, Yet . . . ' " (July/August 1995), and "Always is Always Now" (May/June 1997).

The Christian Ministry, edited by James M. Wall, for "Lord . . . How Often . . . ?" "Salt and Light" (November/December 1991), "The Abomination of Desolation" (March/April 1993), "Requisite Virtue" (May/June 1994), and " 'I Am' " (November/December 1997).

Preaching, edited by Michael Duduit, for "Sharing Our Wounds" (March/April 1994).

The Witness, edited by Jeanie Wylie-Kellermann, for a portion of " 'Will You Carry Me?' " (under the title "Advent's Invitation", December 1991).

The Face of the Deep, edited by Gillian Scharff, for " 'Will You Carry Me?' " (Advent/Christmas/Epiphany 1992-93).

Grateful acknowledgment is also given to *Yankee*, in which the poem "Laude" appeared (May 1992), and to *The Episcopalian: Professional Pages*, in which "Epiphany" appeared (January 1989).

98 99 00 01 02 03 04 05 06 07—10 9 8 7 6 5 4 3 2 1

MANUFACTURED IN THE UNITED STATES OF AMERICA

To the glory of God
and for my parents

Contents

Incarnation

When the Holy One stepped from endless order
into the chaos of our days, it was winter.
Weather blew everywhere. Time itself was dying.
The squirrel, with a tail soft as breath,
curled inside the maple's trunk.

The cold stayed. Five-fingered leaves pressed the ground,
their stems perpendicular, thin wrists above each flame-tipped palm.
Cataclysm scanned the days; like any future, like our own.
The Holy One took face and voice, beginning with an infant cry,
took food and sleep, nestled in arms not unlike yours.

He listened to the dropping rain, watched it bead the naked twigs,
saw it polish stones and faces, stood once beneath this lift of sky
and still, in a word, understands.

Penelope Duckworth

DYNAMIC TEACHING OF THE CHRISTIAN FAITH BUILDS STRONG congregations that make a vital witness. Faithful Christian teaching helps the Christian community respond to the two most important questions in life. Who are we in the light of the gospel? What does the gospel call us to do? The Teaching Sermon Series aims to provide examples of effective teaching sermons.

The time is ripe for a focus on the teaching ministry of the pulpit. Teaching is a prominent emphasis in the preaching of many congregations that are growing in size, in depth of Christian commitment, and in outreach. Teaching sermons appeal to many people today. Further, many contemporary congregations (particularly in the old-line denominations) are declining because they do not have a distinctive sense of Christian identity and mission or a sufficient flow of spiritual energy. Teaching sermons invite diminished churches to the new life that can come when the resources of the gospel, the Bible, Christian tradition, and doctrine are integrated into everyday Christian experience.

The people of God are by nature a teaching community, as Deuteronomy makes clear: "Hear, O Israel: The LORD is our God, the LORD alone. . . . Recite [these words] to your children and talk about them when you are at home and when you are away, when you lie down and when you rise" (Deuteronomy 6:4-7). Teaching is constitutive of the identity of the leaders of the people of God as we recognize by recalling the teaching dimensions of some of the formative ministries of our tradition: Moses, Deborah, Ezra, Jesus, Paul, Priscilla, Origen, Augustine, Catherine of Siena, Luther, Calvin, Wesley, King, Malcolm, McFague, Dozier, Suchocki. A great cloud of witnesses empowers the pastor who would teach from the pulpit.

Teaching sermons have their best effect when they are part of a systemic approach to teaching Christian faith that permeates the

13

Christian community. In the congregational setting, the sermon can play key roles in helping a community develop a consciousness for learning. First, the sermon can be a significant moment of teaching and learning in its own right. The service of worship is the largest regular gathering of the congregation. In a single moment, the preacher has the opportunity to touch the heart, mind, and will of the community. Second, by modeling the vitalization that results from Christian teaching, the sermon can encourage the members of the congregation to take part in the smaller learning groups that are a part of the congregation's life. Third, the sermon can sensitize the congregation to the ways in which the gospel is taught (or not taught) in all that happens in the life of the church.

As I point out in an earlier book, *The Teaching Sermon* (Nashville: Abingdon Press, 1995), there is no single format for teaching sermons. Teaching and learning can take place in multiple ways. Some educational sermons are linear in sequence and informational in tone, while others are associative and evocative. Many teaching sermons combine sequential and associative patterns, as well as analytical and aesthetic approaches. Some teaching sermons center on biblical texts or themes, while others give an interpretation of Christian doctrine, while still others help the congregation reflect on contemporary theological and moral issues. The subjects and methods of Christian teaching are as varied as life itself. The Teaching Sermon Series illustrates the variety in both style and content that is possible when the preacher is a teacher.

Ronald J. Allen

Introduction

IN THE TWENTIETH CENTURY, ROMANO GUARDINI WROTE: "I want no pallid humanitarianism—if Christ be not God, I want none of him; I will hack my way through existence alone. . . ."[1] Sixteen centuries earlier the Council of Nicaea had formulated the doctrine of the Incarnation with its declaration that "Jesus Christ . . . eternally begotten of the Father . . . begotten, not made . . . came down from heaven by the power of the Holy Spirit . . . became incarnate from the Virgin Mary and was made man." Yet, despite being one of the key concepts of the Christian faith, incarnational theology is debated anew age after age. Irenaeus, the vigilant Bishop of Lyons, said, "Among the heretics is always wanting the sentence that the Word of God has become flesh."[2] Consequently, those who would proclaim the Word of God are challenged to find engaging ways to present this doctrine for Christians of the twenty-first century. This collection of sermons is an effort toward that end.

Though Easter is officially the Christian "Queen of Feasts," Christmas appears more dear to both the sacred and secular world, and not simply for commercial reasons. Why should this be so? In many parts of the world Christmas occurs in winter when, perhaps, we are more in need of a festival; perhaps because it is a holiday celebrating the child; or perhaps because Christmas tells us that God came among us as vulnerable as the least of us. To receive God as a child is easier than to celebrate the risen Lord of Easter or anticipate God as our final judge.

The Scottish theologian T. F. Torrance asks, "What would become of this Gospel if there were no oneness of being . . . between Jesus Christ and the Father, if there were at the end no ultimate blending of the forgiving love of Jesus and the final judgments of God? What would it mean for mankind if in the last resort in spite of all the Gospels tell us about Jesus, there is no real bridge in being or nature between him and God?" He concludes, "It would surely mean that in the final analysis Jesus Christ, with all he stands for, is irrelevant for the ultimate destiny of men and women and that the really decisive issues belong to God alone, and to a God whose love fell short of identifying . . . with us."[3]

Torrance's view reminds us that the doctrine of the Incarnation must remain central to a full teaching of the faith, so that Christians may understand the nature of ultimate reality as revealed in Jesus. While God's ways are not human ways and some dimensions of God will always remain unknowable, the evangelist John assures us that Jesus and the Creator God are one. This enables us to put our full trust in the love and grace of the one whose story we know from the Gospels. To paraphrase the Collect for Christmas Day in the *The Book of Common Prayer*, this knowledge gives us joy to receive Christ as our redeemer, and sure confidence to behold him when he comes to be our judge. The Incarnation, while most clearly an Advent, Christmas, and Epiphany theme, can and should be preached throughout the year for evangelism as well as for faith development.

When taught from other seasons of the church year, various facets of the doctrine shine out as different scriptural lessons are examined and proclaimed with the Incarnation in mind. To some, the Incarnation may be a term specifically related to Christ's divinity in relation to his humanity, but my understanding is somewhat broader. Shirley Guthrie, in his book *Christian Doctrine*, expresses such a view: "The content of revelation is a person. God reveals God's self. Revelation is not the giving of some supernatural information about God and human life in the world. It means that God confronts us person-to-person. To receive God's self-revelation is to know not something but someone we did not know before. The revealed truth Christians believe is not an 'it' but a 'thou.' "[4]

The doctrine of the Incarnation makes a powerful claim. It does not say that Jesus was a great man or a major prophet, an ethical ideal or even the center of an archetypal story. What it claims is that Jesus was God Incarnate; that God took on human flesh and dwelt among us. If properly understood, the doctrine of the Incarnation does not make Christians exclusive; on the contrary, the very essence of the doctrine is inviting and inclusive. Genuine inclusivity has a point of reference, while relativism and accommodation are often shifting boundaries.

The theologian Rosemary Haughton confirms the central role of this doctrine when she asks, "What happens if we take Incarnation seriously? There has been a move not only among non-Christians but among many Christians, since the last century, to answer this question by saying, '*Don't* take it seriously; in fact don't take it at all.' " She goes on to say that she believes "the rejection of the idea of Incarnation is not primarily an intellectual decision but an emotional and spiritual revulsion against inadequate (un-poetic) theology and therefore inadequate (un-poetic) Christianity."[5] She sees those refusing incarnational theology doing so because of the lack of articulate exposition.

Because the doctrine of the Incarnation speaks of the mystery of God becoming human, it depends on the felicitous use of language, as mystery is most at home in poetry. When the mystery of the Incarnation is presented in a theology that incorporates poetry, it engages the sense of high romance that inspired Francis of Assisi, Teresa of Avila, Dante, Christina Rossetti, T. S. Eliot, James Weldon Johnson, and others, and that Rosemary Haughton lamented as often missing from contemporary Christianity.

This leads to an additional aspect of the Incarnation that engages and challenges me as a preacher. The linchpin of the doctrine is found in the Prologue to the Gospel of John where the Evangelist proclaims, "The Word became flesh and lived among us" (John 1:14). Cosmic reason, God among us, the *Logos*, is often translated as "the Word," which we also understand as a figure of speech, a means of communication. In *The Book of Common Prayer*, the Rite I Prayer for the Whole State of Christ's Church asks that ministers proclaim God's "true and lively word." "The Word became flesh," and we are asked to proclaim the "lively word."

These phrases establish in my mind an abiding connection between the message or Word of God (in Christ, in Scripture, even in our homiletic efforts) and the enfleshed beings that we are. There is mystery, even mysticism, here. Those who proclaim God's Word have the opportunity and privilege to participate in the Incarnate Word when our words speak the gospel truth in conjunction with the truth of our lives. When such occurs, the liveliness and veracity of the spoken word is transported directly to the bodily life of our hearers. We live out our lives in our bodies, and our bodies respond when our souls are touched. Just as we hunger for physical sustenance, so the soul hungers for nourishment, for the good news that Jesus brought, and souls starve for the lack of it.

The poet Mary Oliver writes:

> And the speck of my heart, in my shed of flesh
> and bone, began to sing out, the way the sun
> would sing if the sun could sing, if light had a
> mouth and a tongue, if the sky had a throat, if
> god wasn't just an idea but shoulders and a spine. . . . [6]

My clearest conviction of the Incarnation is that God took on shoulders and a spine. The Creator became one of us, our kin, our kind, one who understands us. God not only made the earth, but chose to live and die on it as well. It is my hope to proclaim the Incarnation in language befitting such good news.

This collection began as occasional sermons, and the theme became apparent when a thread of continuity was searched out and found. Consequently, the theme is more directly focused in some sermons than in others, but, as it undergirds my theology, it is always there.

A number of people helped in the preparation of this book, and I wish to thank them. First, thanks goes to the Episcopal students of Stanford University and the congregations of nearby Episcopal churches, for whom these sermons were prepared and delivered. Other friends, colleagues, and family members offered immeasurable help and support. They include the Reverend Janna Steed (who first suggested that I send out a sermon for publication and has been a stalwart support ever since); Professor Bernard Silverman, F.R.S.; my mother, Alice Jo Duckworth; my sister, Claudia Duckworth Dorr; and Georgianna Farren, M.D., all of whom read the manuscript and offered excellent suggestions. In addition, Professor Jacob Needleman gave useful direction, Lucy Mack, Professor Daniel Langton, the Reverend Rosemarie Anderson, the Reverend Ruth Eller, and the Very Reverend Alan Jones lent support. I also wish to thank Professor Ronald Allen whose good ideas and enthusiasm have brought it to fruition. Finally, my greatest gratitude goes to my husband, Professor Dennis Gordon, for editorial expertise, help on the home front, and his unfailing, uproarious good humor, and to our daughter, Clare Elizabeth, whose own incarnation gives added meaning to this and every endeavor.

Penelope Duckworth
June 28, 1997
Feast of Irenaeus, Bishop of Lyons

Chapter One

"I Am"

John 4:5-42

A FRIEND ONCE TOLD ME SHE RELISHED GOING to the neighborhood laundromat because in our culture it is the last vestige of the village well. I had never thought of the laundromat in such terms, but it is as good a semblance as we have in contemporary America. The local well has played a central role in many cultures and particularly in stories from the Scriptures. Important things happen there. It was at a well, for example, that Abraham's servant found Rebekah, the wife for Isaac. It was at a well that Jacob met Rachel and fell in love with her. And it was at a well that Moses, fleeing from Pharaoh, met the daughters of the priest of Midian, who gave him sanctuary.

Wells are sources of water, and water has great importance in our faith tradition. In Genesis the Spirit of God hovered over the deep and from the face of the waters called out, "Let there be light" (1:3). From the parting of the Red Sea waters to Jesus' baptism in the Jordan, water has played a crucial role in our spiritual journeys and transformation. Water is moist, fluid, and yielding. It is "yin" in Eastern understanding. In Jungian psychology, it is the feminine, representing the matrix of life, the womb, the oceanic unconscious from which we all come.

In the desert, water is precious. Arab women are said to save their tears because water is so valued. In our Gospel story from John, Jesus comes to a well in Samaria. It is hot, around noon, and he is thirsty. His disciples have gone to the village to buy food, and Jesus waits, alone in the heat of the day. When a woman comes to the well, he asks her if she will draw water for him. Not only was it unusual for a man to speak to a woman he did not know, but Jews did not normally speak to Samaritans.

Let me give you a brief history that will explain this long-standing hostility. When the Assyrians conquered the Northern Kingdom of Israel, they deported most of the Jews and replaced them with people from other countries as a way of demoralizing the Jews and preventing future insurrections. The Samaritans, as these people came to be called, gradually began to worship Yahweh but refused to honor the Temple in Jerusalem and preferred to worship God at altars that they set up in the high hills of Samaria.[1] This generated a hostility between Jews and Samaritans that even their common belief in Yahweh did not mollify.

When the woman asks Jesus why he is speaking to a Samaritan, he answers, "If you knew the gift of God, and who it is that is saying to you, 'Give me a drink,' you would have asked him, and he would have given you living water." The woman responds that the well is deep and asks where he will get the living water. She assumes Jesus means flowing or moving water, as the water in a stream. Jesus explains that the water he gives will be like a natural underground spring. His spring, unlike human constructions, will not run dry or crack its cistern and become useless.

Isaiah welcomed people to this kind of water when he called, "Ho, everyone who thirsts, come to the waters" (55:1). In a sense, it is like the water of the Salinas River that nurtures the fertile farmland of California's central coast yet runs much of its distance unseen beneath the ground. This living water has a source deeper than human knowing but tasted by the great ones of every generation. In his book called *The Well and the Cathedral*, Ira Progoff tells how each stone of a cathedral originally marked the spot where someone made contact with God. The stones accrued and great monuments, traditions, and doctrines were formed. Unfortunately, with such institutional grandeur, we often forget the initial impact that was made. We forget the deep spring of God that underlies such monuments. But if we go down deep enough we will touch that same living water. It remains there and will refresh each of us who goes down to search for it. In the Revelation to John, the Evangelist heard these words, "I am the Alpha and the Omega, the beginning and the end. To the thirsty I will give water as a gift from the spring of the water of life" (21:6).

The early church theologians identified this water with Christ, whom they called "the fountain of life."

The Samaritan woman says to Jesus, "Sir, give me this water, so that I may never be thirsty or have to keep coming here to draw water." The woman still understands Jesus literally and would prefer not to have the burden of drawing water. Jesus responds to her and asks her to go and call her husband. She answers that she has no husband, and Jesus tells her, "You are right in saying, 'I have no husband'; for you have had five husbands, and the one you have now is not your husband. What you have said is true!" This is an interesting exchange and can initially seem like a series of nonsequiturs, but if we look closely and carefully we can see a deeper meaning.

The woman seems to be understanding Jesus only on a literal level. She does not understand that the living water is a relationship with God. She is not aware of her own brokenness and need. By bringing up her broken relationships with men, Jesus is pointing out that her life is not in perfect order.

She then deftly changes the subject, as many of us would do. "Sir," she says, "I see that you are a prophet. Our ancestors worshiped on this mountain; and you say that the place where people must worship is in Jerusalem." The Samaritan woman is uncomfortable and decides to try to engage Jesus on a religious topic, the old Jewish/Samaritan conflict about where God is to be worshiped. But Jesus does not let himself be pulled into the discussion. He skirts the old feud about sites for worship and takes the religious issue to a much deeper level.

He takes the opportunity, when she changes the subject, to teach her things about God that neither she nor her people, nor the Jews for that matter, had considered before. "Woman, believe me, the hour is coming when you will worship the Father neither on this mountain nor in Jerusalem. You worship what you do not know; we worship what we know, for salvation is from the Jews. But the hour is coming, and is now here, when the true worshipers will worship the Father in spirit and truth, for the Father seeks such as these to worship him. God is spirit, and those who worship him must worship in spirit and truth."

Jesus makes two great claims in this passage. First of all he announces that salvation is from the Jews. The Jews made the great monotheistic leap in history and then went on to show how their relationship with God transformed the lives of particular historical individuals. We see this transformation in Abraham, Sarah, Deborah, Joseph, Moses, Miriam, and Elijah, to name a few. These are people who knew God firsthand; they knew the one whom they worshiped. We also see this relationship transform the covenant community through miraculous acts of liberation and preservation.

Second, Jesus proclaims that God is spirit and that God seeks to be worshiped in spirit and truth. As spirit, God can clearly be worshiped anywhere. But Jesus states that God seeks to be worshiped by those whose own spirits are marked by genuine morality and integrity. God is seeking out such individuals whose spirits are kindred to God. It is God's desire that we will find the living water once again and not just rely on the stones and cathedrals and institutions left by others.

The Samaritan woman says, "I know that Messiah is coming" (who is called Christ). "When he comes, he will proclaim all things to us." Once again she tries to dodge the direction of the conversation. She is uncomfortable and says, in effect, *the Messiah is coming and then I won't have to listen to the likes of you*. She no doubt believes that the Messiah will tell her what she wants to hear. To her remark Jesus makes this astonishing reply, "I am he, the one who is speaking to you."

What is even more remarkable is that Jesus doesn't actually say, "I am he; the one who is speaking to you." The original Greek is simply "I am," *ego eimi*, which occurs several times in the Gospel of John. Biblical commentator and Jungian analyst John Sanford says of this passage:

> Biblical scholars call this the "absolute I am," and regard this Greek construction as both grammatically peculiar and extremely important. The reason for its importance is that in the Old Testament, when Moses asks God whom he shall tell the people has told him these things, God says to him, "Say to the Israelites, 'I am has sent me to you'" (Exod. 3:14). The phrase *ego eimi* is the Greek equivalent expression for the Hebrew phrase translated as "I am." Thus Jesus is using the sacred name of God with reference to himself.[2]

Here is the doctrine of the Incarnation in two words: "I am," uttered first by the liberating God of Exodus and again by Jesus to a Samaritan woman beside a well.

The poet Christopher Smart wrote:

> God all-bounteous, all-creative,
> Whom no ills from good dissuade,
> Is incarnate, and a native
> Of the very world he made.[3]

Imagine: the great Creator who fashioned the heavens and earth has come among us in the person of Jesus Christ, and made you and me to reflect that same creative image. God became a native of the very world God made.

Our story continues. The disciples return to Jesus with no idea of what has happened. The woman hurries back to the city and tells her neighbors of Jesus. Despite her resistance, Jesus has had a tremendous impact on her and she proves to be an evangelist of some skill, bringing many people to "come and see a man who told me everything I have ever done."

When the woman left Jesus to go and tell her neighbors, she left her water jar at the well. She may have done this because carrying a full jar on her head would have slowed her down and she had exciting news to tell. It may have been that she left it for the disciples' use. But I suspect that she left it for another reason. I suspect that, in spite of herself, she had tasted some of the living water that Jesus offered her and forgot the well water for which she came. Or perhaps, like those others who tasted living water and left stones to mark the place, she left what she had to mark the place where she had tasted water from the fountain of life and met God Incarnate face to face.

Chapter Two

"Learn from Me"

| Matthew 11:25-30 | CHILDHOOD IS A BRIEF, PRECARIOUS, AND precious time. Those of us who are parents watch with amazement as the chubby, |

wobbly legs stretch tall and the tentative first words evolve into full-fledged conversation. The Gospel lesson tells us that childhood is also instructive in our faith and that children offer us a unique way of knowing God. In this passage from Matthew, Jesus thanks God for the understanding that is hidden from the learned and revealed to children. Jesus speaks of the knowledge of God that comes to us when we are like children, in a childlike frame of mind. Elsewhere he said we must become as children to enter God's kingdom (Mark 10:15).

He is speaking of the special quality that children have that is often lost as we enter adulthood. Practitioners of Zen call it beginner's mind. Mystics speak of the cloud of unknowing. It is an emptiness, an awareness of need, an openness, a wonder. Understood in this way, children seem closer to a remembered heaven. Such an open state of being allows us to be open to revelation. The experience of poverty or bereavement, of imprisonment or the realization of personal inadequacy can prompt us to such a state, as can the crises of moving through life's transitions. Jesus commends that state of being and urges us to find it in ourselves or to join those who are there.

Let me give you an example of one who had such an open awareness of God. In 1960 six-year-old Ruby Bridges went to first grade in the William Franz Elementary School in New Orleans. She was the first African-American child to integrate the all-white school and she walked with federal marshals past hostile, jeering crowds.

For weeks that turned into months she walked past threatening adults and children, carrying her lunch box and school satchel to go into an empty classroom in an empty building. She was the only child there. But she had a sunny disposition and worked hard and was supported by her parents and her church community.

Her teacher worried about her and questioned her, but Ruby said she was doing fine and she seemed to be. Then one morning her teacher noticed that Ruby did something different. She stopped in front of the angry crowd and seemed to be talking to them. The crowd got angrier and the marshals tried to hurry Ruby, but she wouldn't budge. When Ruby came into the classroom, her teacher asked her what she had said to the people in the crowd. Ruby said she had not spoken to the people. Her teacher persisted. Ruby insisted that she had not talked to them. Her teacher said she had seen Ruby's lips moving. "I wasn't talking," Ruby said. "I was praying. I was praying for them."

Every day Ruby had stopped and prayed on her way to school. That morning she had forgotten until she saw the crowd, and so she said her prayers then and there. Eventually, her classmates came back and Ruby was able to continue her schooling like other children. But during her ordeal her relationship with God had sustained her.[1] Jesus said, "I thank you, Father, Lord of heaven and earth, because you have hidden these things from the wise and the intelligent and revealed them to infants; yes, Father, for such was your gracious will."

Now it seems to be part of adult human nature to resist that state of need and emptiness where revelation is most likely to occur, and yet life pushes us there at almost every juncture. Think of the toddler, the school-age kid on the first day of school, the adolescent, young parents, those in midlife crises, empty nesters, workers laid off from long-term jobs, recent retirees, widows and widowers, those facing disability or death. All of these are in a state of crisis which is also a state of opportunity. It is a place where our sense of ourselves and our sense of God is immediate and open to renewal. Jesus commends such places of need and urges us to go there voluntarily.

In our culture we spend vast amounts of money and time in a tremendous effort to have control over our lives. But life continues to offer us situations we cannot control. We are thrown time and again into dependency on God, and most of us are uncomfortable

there. We like to feel empowered and independent. We like the
familiar comforts of our known world and we want to stay where we
are; but when we do, we actually are not staying in the same place
but are moving farther and farther from a vibrant connection with
God. It is the saints who most often point us in the direction back
toward God. Francis of Assisi is a good example (and our Gospel
from Matthew is also the one appointed for his feast). We catch a
glimpse of the saint's perspective in these lines of poetry:

> Saint Francis fell in love with loss
> he courted emptiness and absence
> he called it Lady, spent his days
> and nights in search of lacking more.
> He would have found her in each loss
> he would have loved the empty hand
> the end of line that brought in nothing.
>
> Surely his dreams in spangled darkness
> enticed and beckoned. Still, he left them
> desiring the rising morning light,
> its rich and recent emptiness.[2]

To live is to grow and change. And to grow and change means to
comprehend God in different ways. As we progress through life, we
come to understand God in new ways as our own lenses change. Each
transition we undergo feels at first like a loss. We are thrown into a crisis.
But it is only by going through the loss, and the feelings of personal
emptiness, that the crisis becomes an opportunity for new growth and
understanding. It is through such transitions that we gain a deeper
understanding of God, and it is helpful to remember that our Lord
experienced human growth and change in his time among us.

Years ago, when I was in seminary, I took a class at the Jesuit School
of Theology in Berkeley. The class was titled "The Will of God as
the Ultimate Moral Standard." We were asked to write a paper on a
particular ethical decision and show how God's will, as it was understood, was a factor in the personal decision-making process. I initially
chose to write about the decision of Dietrich Bonhoeffer, a young
Lutheran pastor in Nazi Germany, to become part of a plot to kill
Hitler.

I went to talk with the professor and, to my surprise, he asked me a number of questions about myself and my own faith journey. Eventually, I found myself telling him about a particularly difficult time in my life when my sense of God had changed from a childhood's faith to something wooden and dead, and then to some incomprehensible and relentless otherness, and finally to a painful silence that over time was revealing a comforting presence.

He asked me not to write about Dietrich Bonhoeffer but rather to write about the crisis I had undergone and my new understanding of God. I did as he asked, and the paper flowed effortlessly from my experience. Years later I realized that if I had not been asked to reflect on that difficult time, to put it into language and write it down, painful as it was, I might not have come to value it as a turning point in my life, an experience that matured and deepened my faith. It might have remained a collage of nonverbal impressions logged in my mind along with the daily experiences of a forgotten year. Through that class I came to understand that God acts in my own history and reaches out to me in times of emptiness and need.

Our Gospel text speaks of ways of knowing God. One of the Latin roots of the word *education* means to be led forth and to branch out. Having served as a chaplain at a variety of institutions of higher learning, I have found that many understand education as the acquiring of information, rather than being drawn into fuller personhood. For me this distinction is a false dichotomy. Ideally our education consists of the acquisition of facts and the mastery of skills and technology, as well as the development of critical thinking and our God-given insight and understanding.

The scripture text continues with these words of Jesus, "All things have been handed over to me by my Father; and no one knows the Son except the Father, and no one knows the Father except the Son and anyone to whom the Son chooses to reveal him." It is a passage that sounds more like the Gospel of John than the Synoptic Gospels. It is a statement of God becoming human that is second only to the great incarnational text from the first chapter of the Gospel of John, "the Word became flesh and dwelt among us" (John 1:14 RSV). But it also speaks of knowing: "no one *knows* the Father except the Son and anyone to whom the Son chooses to reveal him."[3] Again it speaks of a kind of knowledge that is revelatory.

"Remember that Christianity is not, first and foremost, a religion; it is first and foremost a revelation,"[4] urged Archbishop William Temple. "Revelation means knowledge as grace," writes Frederick Buechner. He goes on to say, "No one has ever managed to *find out* much of anything about God. . . . Nobody figured Christianity out. It happened. That is what it means to call it a *revealed* religion—not incompatible with reason maybe, if you give it some thought, but not arrived at primarily by reason either."[5]

Our Gospel reading concludes with the invitation, "Come to me, all you that are weary and are carrying heavy burdens, and I will give you rest. Take my yoke upon you, and learn from me; for I am gentle and humble in heart, and you will find rest for your souls. For my yoke is easy, and my burden is light."

Is there any among us who is not "heavy laden"? Whether it is the weight of potential or ambition, worry or fear, all of us come to this altar with burdens. Whether we bring a cross of pain, a hunger to know God, a fear of emptiness, a burden of guilt, or just a chip on our shoulder, we are invited to set down our load. We are summoned to join with our Savior who is lowly and gentle, who will soon nourish us in the Holy Eucharist with his own body and blood. He who has searched us out and known us requests that we remember our wonder. He who loves us as we are tells us to learn from his example. He invites us to exchange our heavy burdens for easy ones, and he will take ours and shoulder them to glory in the shape of his cross.

Chapter Three

"Will You Carry Me?"

Luke 1:39-56   NOT LONG AGO AT A CATHOLIC WORKER IN-fant House, a shelter for battered and abused children, a small boy of about five was to be placed in a foster home. The woman who runs the house was walking him out to the car to meet his new foster parents when the boy, who had grown to feel very secure in his time at the shelter, asked her, "Will you carry me?" The woman reached down to reassure him and said she thought he was getting a little too big to be carried. The boy responded by saying, "I mean in your heart." The woman was surprised that the small child spoke so figuratively and told him that she certainly would. As he got nearer the car he said, "Will you remember to kiss me good night?" This time she knew he was not speaking literally and so she said she would; she would remember him each night, and she would carry him in her heart.

This story illustrates what is being asked of us in the pregnant time of Advent. Much is being asked of us: We are asked to carry the embryonic Christ in our hearts and to prepare for his coming again. We are asked to make room for him, to prepare a home so he will not always be consigned to the stable. And we are asked to compre-hend that strong and mystical commingling in which we know ourselves and others to be a part of a divine and eternal life, the Body of Christ.

In the Gospel, both Mary and Elizabeth are confident that Mary will bear the Christ Child. While Joseph may yet be unsure, these two women are convinced of Mary's participation in God's will. And not only is Elizabeth sure, but the baby in her womb, the one who will become John the Baptist, gives her significant notice as well.

As you recall, Mary's first response to the news of Gabriel was one of fear, but she soon overcame her fear and gave a clear response, "Here am I, the servant of the Lord; let it be with me according to your word" (Luke 1:38). The whole wonderful story that we retell at Advent is not one of logical sequence. It is a long and complex story full of angels and disbelief, prophets and unlikely births. It appears that one way we can prepare a place for Christ is to be ready for the unexpected, simply to allow the unplanned into our lives. Madeleine L'Engle wrote:

> This is the irrational season,
> When love blooms bright and wild.
> Had Mary been filled with reason,
> There'd have been no room for the child.[1]

The logic of God may seem quite foreign to us, but divine reason, the *Logos,* will come if we make room for God in our lives. Then, for whatever reason or "unreason," we can proclaim with the old English carol:

> Behold the great Creator makes himself a house of clay;
> A robe of human flesh he takes that he will wear for e'er.[2]

The logic of God challenges us right away for God chose a virgin birth as a means of coming into the world. While this concept may seem a physiological stumbling block to some, the psychological truth is clear, and this psychological truth applies to each of us: the Christ will be conceived and born in us through no less than the hand of God. Each and every time one of us finds or is found by God, a new being emerges and this is a miracle no human hands have wrought. Each of us can be understood as the sum and result of our personal evolution until we are touched by God; then something different has entered our lives and someone new is born. We can easily explain evil acts by looking at the history of the perpetrator, but when someone does something remarkably generous or courageous, persons such as Mother Teresa and Archbishop Tutu, they are usually the first to ascribe their reasons to God. As Frederick Buechner says, "Evil . . . evolves. Only holiness happens."[3]

Mary and Elizabeth demonstrate the belief that God acts in history, and they show the kind of faith necessary to bring about the reign of Christ. But that is not all they tell us; they also speak of the implications of bearing the Christ into our world and our times.

In Elizabeth, Mary has found the family member and friend who understands what is happening to her, and Elizabeth accepts, affirms, and rejoices with Mary in her great, frightening calling. As is often the case when our friends give us affirmation, we are empowered. So Mary summons words from her recollection of the Scriptures and spills forth her joy and perception of what is happening in the words of the Magnificat.

She reaches far back in the Jewish tradition and echoes the words that Hannah used at the birth of Samuel (1 Sam. 2:1-10). She chooses the words of another woman, and these lovely and terrible words speak no less than revolution. Her words are words of comfort for the oppressed, but they are frightening words for the rich and the powerful. She says of God, "He has shown strength with his arm; he has scattered the proud in the thoughts of their hearts. He has brought down the powerful from their thrones, and lifted up the lowly; he has filled the hungry with good things, and sent the rich away empty." If she used this same song as a sort of lullaby, we might more clearly understand its echo in the Beatitudes found later in Luke, "Blessed are you who are hungry now, for you will be filled. . . . Woe to you who are full now, for you will be hungry" (Luke 6:21-26).

So often we think of Mary as the gentle and obedient bride-to-be, or as the vulnerable, unwed teenager, but the Mary of the Magnificat is a very different woman. For centuries this passage of Scripture has been recited in the monastic tradition ushering in the evening, and it is a central point of the beautiful Anglican service of Evensong. It continues to tell us of God who has a preference for the poor and who requires us to "do justice, and to love kindness, and to walk humbly" (Micah 6:8) with our God. It also speaks to us of the confidence of the young woman who will participate, by giving birth, in turning the world and the powers of the world upside down.

The twelfth chapter of the book of the Revelation is not commonly read during Advent, but I would like to add it to our Scripture readings. Listen to portions of it:

> A great portent appeared in heaven: a woman clothed with the sun, with the moon under her feet, and on her head a crown of twelve stars. She was pregnant and was crying out in birth pangs, in the agony of giving birth. Then another portent appeared in heaven: a great red dragon, with seven heads and ten horns, and seven diadems on his heads. . . . Then the dragon stood before the woman who was about to bear a child, so that he might devour her child as soon as it was born. And she gave birth to a son. . . . But her child was snatched away and taken to God and to his throne; and the woman fled into the wilderness. . . . And war broke out in heaven; Michael and his angels fought against the dragon. The dragon and his angels fought back, but they were defeated. . . . The great dragon was thrown down, that ancient serpent, who is called the Devil and Satan, the deceiver of the whole world—he was thrown down to the earth, and his angels were thrown down with him. . . . So when the dragon saw that he had been thrown down to the earth, he pursued the woman who had given birth to the male child. . . . But the earth came to the help of the woman. . . . Then the dragon was angry with the woman, and went off to make war on the rest of her children, those who keep the commandments of God and hold the testimony of Jesus.

The woman in the Revelation gives birth while looking into the eye of the dragon. The birth of her child promises a new reign other than that which the dragon holds. She is very vulnerable; and her life, as well as her child's life, is at stake. But she goes on creating a new world in the face of a raging and furious old order.

The book of the Revelation is full of cosmic imagery. The woman is crowned with twelve stars, as in the twelve tribes of Israel, and the dragon has seven heads and ten horns, with the horn being a symbol of authority and command, and the multitude of horns being power running amuck. This dragon is a very political beast. While the dragon has been interpreted to be any one of a variety of different regimes, it is not limited to any particular history. The dragon is the power behind the powers, the one who goes by many names: the accuser, the deceiver, the destroyer, the confuser, the seducer, the evil one, death. And this power, this dragon, is on watch for any advent of new birth.

Bill Kellermann, writing in *Sojourners* magazine, portrays the woman in the passage, the Queen of Heaven, as the embodiment of the justice proclaimed in the Magnificat. She is the cosmic Mary, an extension of the young woman we meet in the Gospels. He writes of her encounter with the dragon, "The woman looks it in the eye. And at the heavenly heart of things, it is already defeated, though not without a bitter fight. Before the woman, against the Incarnation, the dragon takes up a stance that is a twisted parody of Advent. It watches. It is alert and awake, crouched and ready, preparing in its own fashion for the child's arrival."[4]

We see clearly the flexing muscles of the powers-that-were in the events around the Christmas story: Joseph and Mary went to be taxed because Caesar Augustus conducted surveillance and wanted to keep tabs on everyone. Beyond Caesar's repression, we see the dragon's sinister nature when Herod cannot find the newborn child, the King of the Jews who, he believes, threatens his power, and so he launches the "slaughter of the innocents." The dragon will do anything to maintain its power. The beginning of a new and just reign, the coming of the kingdom of God, threatens the dragon's hold on the world.

Still, the woman will give birth and the child will be caught up to God. But this will enrage and incense the dragon who will continue to try to destroy the woman and her life-giving potential. When it cannot destroy her, it will continue to make war on humanity, especially on those who witness to Christ, those who try to carry God's Word into the world.

On the last Sunday of Advent, Christ is once more coming into the world. But he does not come into a Christmas-card world of gentle beasts and hovering angels. He comes into a world as war-torn and as unjust as the one he originally entered twenty centuries ago. He comes into a world where powers and authorities still stifle and kill to maintain their power and prestige. He comes into a world where there is great manipulation of ideologies to maintain power and where the world and all life on it are hostage to the ancient principle of death, only modernized to fit our technological age.

But Christ will come because there are some courageous enough to look death in the eye and still push for new life. Christ will come and will find scant room in our world once more. He will come and find that he must once again flee the dragon, or the powers-that-be, and become a refugee like so many in our times. He will come in poverty and remind us that God has a preference for the poor and oppressed. The dragon will chase and harass him until he will finally confront its full force, which is death, and then he will overcome it. But I am getting ahead of the story.

The main message of this time and of our Gospel is that Christ is coming again and, like a child, he looks for us to help him come into our world. "Will you carry me?" he says, and we look out and see imprinted on the world the face of a dragon that will try to devour us and any new life we may bring. It will do so in a thousand ways: in cynicism, in ridicule, in inattention, and in many forms of violence. We must be prepared for such a response. For as Paul says, "our struggle is not against enemies of blood and flesh, but against the rulers, against the authorities, against the cosmic powers of this present darkness, against the spiritual forces of evil in the heavenly places" (Eph. 6:12). But there are other powers that, in the wild logic of God, will come to our aid: powers of love and hope and gentleness. The Spanish poet Antonio Machado wrote:

> From the door sill of a dream they called my name. . . .
> It was the good voice, the voice I loved so much.
>
> "—Listen: will you go with me to visit the soul? . . . "
> A soft stroke reached up to my heart.
>
> "With you always" . . . And in my dream I walked
> down a long and solitary corridor,
> aware of the touching of the pure robe,
> and of the soft beating of blood in the hand that loved me.[5]

The very first Advent began in a Galilean springtime, when God asked a young woman if she literally would carry the Christ and bear him into the world. Each Advent, the Christ Child asks us, asks again and again because at some point we are always beginning, "Will you carry me? Will you carry me in your heart? Will you carry me and remember to kiss me good night?"

Chapter Four

Gifts and Revelations

Matthew 2:1-12

TWELFTH NIGHT IS THE LAST OF
Christmas, the last night of the season of
gift-giving, and the Eve of Epiphany in which
we celebrate the original gift-giving, the gifts of the Magi, whose
example is the reason we give gifts at Christmas.

I want to tell you a story about gifts. Before the Pilgrims landed
in this country, the native peoples had a tradition: they would
circulate the sacred peace pipe among the local tribes. It would stay
in a certain lodge for a time but sooner or later would be given away
again. When the English came, they were invited to share the sacred
pipe, as was the custom. The leading settler immediately took the
peace pipe and put it on the mantel in his cabin. There it stayed and
stayed and stayed. After a long time, the native people came to visit.
It was apparent that they expected something. Finally, a translator
explained that the Englishman should offer them a smoke and give
them the pipe. The Englishman was disgruntled. Clearly the natives
didn't understand private property, and the term "Indian-giver" was
coined.[1]

We have inherited a European understanding of gifts. We keep
gifts that we receive. I suggest to you that Jesus was more like the
native people in the story. Jesus could be called an "Indian-giver" in
that he wanted gifts to circulate, to keep on giving.

Let's look at the Gospel story for this night. We learn that wise
ones from the East have come looking for the one who has been born

King of the Jews. They had seen a star in the east and had followed it. The Magi were probably Zoroastrians from Persia. They were seekers after truth, more like priests than kings (except insofar as each of us is a king or queen in the center of our being). They were rulers in the realm of knowledge. In them the world's oldest knowledge paid homage to Christ.

They knew from the stars that something extraordinary was occurring, and the unusual conjunction of Jupiter and Saturn pointed to Palestine for an explanation. And so they set forth and consulted Herod, who, after conferring with the chief priests and scribes, sent the Magi to Bethlehem, for prophecy had designated this ancient city as the site of the Messiah's birth. They found the infant Jesus with his mother, and they fell on their knees and worshiped him. Then they offered him their gifts: gold, frankincense, and myrrh.

These gifts which were given to the Christ Child—gold, frankincense, and myrrh—are the gifts that Jesus continues to circulate. Let me explain. The first is gold, the shining, pure, true metal, the stuff of coronets and wedding bands, of royalty and fidelity. It is the metal most valued, what was for centuries the backing of financial exchange, and is for many today the epitome of "hard currency." It is foremost a means of wealth. Jesus asks us to share our wealth, to give to the poor and the needy. He understood the righteous as those who share their food and clothing and shelter (the things that money buys) with those in need. He wants the gift of gold to keep on giving.

The second gift is frankincense, a gum resin that is burnt to provide scented smoke used for the purification of holy things, holy people, and holy places. Jesus extended holiness beyond the official religiosity of the day. He told the Pharisees that tax collectors and prostitutes would precede them into God's kingdom. He expands the aromatic aura of sanctity to include ordinary sinners like most of us. He wants to enfold and engulf all of us in the reign of God.

The last gift is myrrh, a bitter perfumed extract that was used for sacred anointing and preparation for burial. It has also been used in medicine and is thought to have healing properties. Each of us symbolically dies with Christ at our baptism, and we are then born into new life. And each of us is anointed at baptism or confirmation and marked as Christ's own forever. Through the gift of the death and resurrection of Christ, we are a kingdom of priests. We are called to heal the sick and raise the dead and trust in the promise of eternal life.

This is truly the season of gifts. In addition to celebrating the Twelfth Night of Christmas, we also begin the Feast of Epiphany or, as it used to be called, the Manifestation of Christ to the Gentiles. This is the time when Christ was made manifest among us, as vulnerable as a newborn and as imperiled as a refugee. Tonight begins the season of Epiphany, a period recounting and encouraging revelations, new understandings of God, lights in the darkness. It is a time to think about how we know God and how we can know God more deeply.

This is the season of lights, stars, dreams. You remember that God warned the Magi not to return to Herod by a dream, and Joseph protected the Christ Child through messages he received in his dreams. God comes to us in many ways and in many forms. How do you know God? How has God been revealed to you? Think back. Was it a time of joy, fullness, laughter? Or was it one of loss or sorrow, when you surrendered yourself to another's care? Maybe it was both. Was it through a friend? Your true love? A pilgrimage? A child? A stranger? A dream?

This poem, called "Epiphany," speaks of one way God became known.

> Our gifts were lavish
> to be sure,
> especially in that stable
> where food and warmth
> were scarce enough.
> But it wasn't my gift
> that mattered;
> it was more the going.
>
> Something happened on the road,
> the place between,
> where I had no boundaries.
> I found and lost
> such different things.
> And it was that releasing,

the having then letting go,
that I came to treasure.

It was only emptiness
but the best I had to offer.
So after all the other gifts,
I gave it to him in the shadows,
a tiny well of emptiness,
as weak as all beginning,
and he received me there within it
as if it were his home.[2]

We all have different experiences and different ways we have known God. What is yours?

Perhaps it was long ago, so long that it feels remote, unreal. Perhaps you had hoped to draw near again this Christmas but got lost in wrapping paper and ribbons, last-minute sales, cards, travel, and parties. Maybe it was family issues, "the hopes and fears of all the years" that converged again and obscured the Christ Child. It is no accident that there was no room at the inn. The story repeats itself for many of us.

I marvel at the wisdom of our forebears that proclaimed a full twelve days of Christmas. There is still time, not much, but a little. There are still gifts circulating—abundant, extravagant, well-loved gifts. Give them. Take them. They are for you. Maybe revelation is a gift waiting to be unwrapped.

Theodore Roethke once wrote:

A lively understandable spirit
Once entertained you.
It will come again.
Be still.
Wait.[3]

There are as many revelations as stars in the skies. They call us from our busy, ordered days to go outside beneath the spangled heavens: to listen, to look and then to run with shepherds and kneel with kings.

Chapter Five

The Incarnate Word

O God, you have given us the gift of speech and language, and have revealed your purpose to us through the same; let your Word move among the words spoken this day in your name that they may bear, albeit brokenly, the mark of your truth. Amen.

John 1:1-18

THE FOURTH GOSPEL OF THE NEW TESTAMENT offers a new beginning. "In the beginning was the Word." After a long history of failure and faithfulness, persecution and promise, the people of God are given a fresh start. These phrases echo the words of Genesis. This new beginning is redolent of God's great beginning acts, and its purpose is to restore the original shape and intention to creation. But this beginning is more than earth and sky, element and creature, it is the beginning of wisdom and understanding. "In the beginning was the Word." A Word beyond etymology and philology, this Word is the life and light of humanity. This Word has the power to make us new creatures and to give us new life.

The original Greek for "Word" in the Gospel reading is *Logos*. We understand that it means language, but language infused with truth, order, and wisdom. The Word of God is to God what a person's word is to herself or to himself. That word is almost another entity, the means through which a person acts, by which she or he is expressed.

It is through the Word, through prophets, and through wisdom, that God is made manifest in human history.

And the Word was made flesh. The Word was Jesus. Jesus is not only one who speaks words and makes language; Jesus becomes the very Word that is divine. The evangelist John does not tell us of Jesus' human beginning, of stable and star, manger and Magi. He leaves that to the other Gospels. Rather, he tells the origin of Christ from the perspective of the Godhead. John also differs from the other evangelists in that he combines narrative with metaphor and theology. And the first and great metaphor he uses is that of the Word. The Swiss theologian Hans Urs von Balthasar says, "Jesus Christ is the Word. He is the word and language as such, the word and the speech of God in the word and speech of [human beings]." He continues, "The form of his word carries its own conviction, just as much as, and even more than, the words of a great poet are their own witness. . . . Praise and blame will pass away, but the words of Shakespeare will not pass away. Equally, and even more so, is the word of God."[1]

Our words show our perception of the world, as when the ancient Hebrew poet wrote, "For everything there is a season, and a time for every matter under heaven" (Eccles. 3:1). It is our word that creates the everyday bonds of community, as when the merchant says, "I'll have that for you on Saturday." It is also our word which expresses our integrity; for example, when a military officer says to another, "No, I cannot do that"; or when a woman says to a man, "I, Sara, take you, James, to be my husband"; or when a witness solemnly swears to "tell the truth, the whole truth, and nothing but the truth. . . . "

When our word is broken or is incomplete, when it loses connection with our own center of being, then our relationships become confused and chaotic and the community we have built deteriorates. Human community dissolves when our words do not speak our hearts. In Dante's *Divine Comedy*, those who have broken or betrayed their words, those who practiced deceit or fraud were found in the lowest reaches of hell.

Jesus spoke the truth. But Jesus was more than the integrity of his language. Jesus was the language or Word of God. He came to heal fully that breach between speech and heart. The heart and voice became one in him and he showed us how to keep the two together:

through faithfulness, through suffering, through authenticity. When Jesus said, "Your sins are forgiven," "Your faith has made you well," "Today, salvation has come to this house," his words were the reality. There was no hypocrisy in his speech.

Almost all of us know the pain of being betrayed by language: by broken promises, lies, false witness, hurtful gossip. All of us know our deep attachment to the truth and meaning of words, whether those of others or our own. And yet our postmodern ears are wary and weary of language that often conceals as much as it reveals. Cynicism and distrust of words abound. We see words manipulated for power and profit, and lying has become almost institutionalized by many politicians and corporate executives.

Not long ago I was reading a sermon by Bishop Lancelot Andrewes, the great Jacobean preacher, and I came across an interesting piece of information. He pointed out that the Hebrew word for "flesh," *basar*, and the Hebrew word for "good tidings," *besorah*, have a common root.[2] Now this is interesting because at the very inception of language there was a perceived linkage between word and flesh. We might wonder how this could come about: Surely the birth of a child is good news, something to shout about. Or, to look at it another way, once a word is out, it has taken on a life of its own. It is enfleshed. But I believe that our ancestors, the ancient philologers, those who first coined words, knew that language which speaks the heart is of itself good news.

But how do we come to speak such language? In a world suffused with deceit and the misuse of language, how do we make our speech authentic? How do we speak our heart? How do we enable the incarnate Word to be born in us? The answer is deceptively simple. We listen. We quiet our own egotistical urge to speak until we have listened. We listen to God, to other human beings around us, and to our own hearts. Jacob Needleman terms the speech of the heart "intentional speech." He writes, "Intentional speech almost always costs something to the speaker, that is, it is rooted in some kind of inner sacrifice, inner renunciation. It is *not* the kind of speaking that is more properly called talking and that wastes so much of our life. . . . Talking can be filled with emotion or it can convey a great deal of knowledge and thought. But it becomes speech only when it is intentional, and it is intentional only when we struggle against the momentum of unconscious self-concealment upon which so much of our lives and our sense of self is based."[3]

Such speech is akin to the incarnate Word of God. It is like the speech that made the hearers of Jesus say he spoke with authority, unlike the scribes and Pharisees. It is speech that goes from heart to heart, and when we have experienced such speech something new comes about. Most of us have encountered such speech at least once in our lives. They are words that resonate deep within the heart's core. We may have said them ourselves or someone may have said them to us. However they came, we are changed, healed, transformed.

Emily Dickinson, whose speech was most intentional, wrote:

> A word is dead
> When it is said,
> Some say.
> I say it just
> Begins to live
> That day.[4]

The Christian journey is toward the Word made flesh, both in comprehending the great mystery of the Incarnation of Christ and in our own lives and speech. God is ever creating and re-creating, seeking to give us a new unity of heart and voice. The power of God is at work in truthful words, loving words, healing words.

Let us listen for and pronounce such words for the ongoing glory of God. In doing so, we once again enable the Word to become flesh and dwell among us.

Chapter Six

Requisite Virtue

Micah 6:1-8

THE WORD *VIRTUE* SOUNDS PECULIARLY OUT-
dated in contemporary society. It conjures up a
bygone era. Cicero's phrase "Virtue is its own
reward" brings up images of prudery and of crusaders like Carrie
Nation. And yet we lament the loss of ethical conduct in our culture
and most sadly in our public servants. We become inured to deceit
and fraud in high places and are pleasantly surprised when we find
vestiges of decency in our own business dealings.

No, clearly virtue did not go out of fashion along with Victorian
bustles and high-buttoned shoes. The word just suffers from benign
neglect and is lightly sleeping in our time. It has a long and distin-
guished history both in our church and, earlier, in the classical world.

I would like to talk with you about virtue because it is virtue that
forms our character. We don't hear much talk about excellence of
character, but we all long for it and grieve the absence of it in our
daily lives. Essentially, character means the personality formed with
a view toward goodness, and virtues are goodness differentiated into
various areas of human life.

The Greeks singled out four virtues that have come down to us as
the cardinal virtues: wisdom, courage, temperance, and justice. The
medieval church accepted these four as the natural virtues but added
faith, hope, and charity as the supernatural or theological virtues.
Then things got a bit more complicated: along came the seven deadly
sins, and their concomitant virtues followed. If we go on and consider
the nine fruits of the spirit that Paul lists in Galatians (5:22-23), we
have a fairly long list.

Our Old Testament lesson from Micah is a call to virtue. In it the prophet dismisses the major sacrificial possibilities of the faithful in their efforts to please and appease God. After a barrage of questions, we can almost hear his voice raise to thunder as he says, "He has told you, O mortal, what is good; and what does the Lord require of you but to do justice, and to love kindness, and to walk humbly with your God?"

To do justice is to render to each his or her due. Justice is one of the cardinal virtues from ancient times. We have a powerful example of one who did justice in the late Thurgood Marshall. Marshall knew oppression firsthand and never forgot it. He continued, despite the honors and comforts of his life on the Supreme Court, to work for those who were neglected by the law.

Now, most of us are not justices or judges, but we can still do justice in our daily lives. We can be fair and impartial in our business dealings, we can work for those suffering injustice or oppression, and we can uphold the laws of our society (unless they are patently unjust, in which case we are obliged to protest). A virtue and a capacity we can all attain, justice requires an equanimity of judgment, which is the product of prayer and clear thinking.

Micah also calls us to love kindness. If we love kindness, we love that which binds us, and I think we can fairly call such love "charity." Charity is one of the three theological virtues and was deemed the greatest of the three by Paul in his well-known passage from Corinthians: "And now abideth faith, hope, charity, these three; but the greatest of these is charity" (1 Cor. 13:13 KJV).

We all know that there are different kinds of love, and C. S. Lewis took the time to sort them out. He arrived at four kinds of love: the love we feel for the familiar, love for our friends, erotic love, and the undeserved love that imitates the love of God. It is this last love, called *agape*, that we translate as charity, and those of us who have ever received this love know it to be no poor sister to the other three so-called natural affections. It is, in fact, the strongest of them all, and it alone can pierce even the hardest human heart.[1]

Oscar Wilde wrote of a man who raised his hat to him as Wilde walked by in chains on his way to trial. He said, "When wisdom has been profitless to me, philosophy barren, and the proverbs and phrases of those who have sought to give me consolation as dust and ashes in my mouth, the memory of that little, lovely, silent act of love has unsealed for me all the wells of pity; brought me out of the bitterness of lonely exile into harmony with the wounded, broken, and great heart of the world."[2]

Charity or kindness acknowledges our underlying kinship to one another. It is loving our neighbor as ourselves. Once when Henry James was saying good-bye to his nephew he said something the child never forgot. "There are three things that are important in human life," James avowed. "The first is to be kind. The second is to be kind. The third is to be kind."[3]

Finally, Micah asks us to walk humbly with our God. Essentially he is calling us to the virtue of humility. Sometimes we can understand something like humility better by looking at its opposite; so let us look for a moment at pride, the most lethal of the seven deadly sins. You may recall that Adam and Eve were tempted by Satan, who told them, "You will be like God, knowing good and evil" (Gen. 3:5). Adam and Eve succumbed to temptation in order to be as gods. The Greek word *hubris* means pride so great that the bearer arrogates to himself or herself the power of the gods. The root of pride is our desire for the power of God and as such gives rise to the rest of the deadly sins. It places our own desires above all else. You may also remember that Lucifer, though foremost among the angels, wanted to be like God. He was cast from heaven to the earth. The desire to be God is the original sin. All of us have tried to do it.

In the *Divine Comedy*, Dante places the proud on the lowest cornice of Purgatory where they walk around the holy mountain with huge stones on their backs. The stones force them to look down at the ground at the humus, the earth, from which our word *humility* comes.[4] Humility is the antidote for pride: to be of the earth, to keep our eyes on the dust from which we came and to which we will return.

Frederick Buechner said, "True humility doesn't consist of thinking ill of yourself but of not thinking of yourself much differently from the way you'd be apt to think of anybody else. It is the capacity for being no more and no less pleased when you play your own hand well than when your opponents do."[5] Or as Francis of Assisi said, "Let your privilege be to have no privilege."[6]

In Matthew 5:1-12, Jesus teaches the Beatitudes and we see a further extension of these virtues. To be poor in spirit, to mourn, to be meek, are all examples and consequences of humility. To thirst for righteousness and to be merciful are extensions of justice. And to acquire purity of heart, to be a peacemaker, and to endure persecution for the sake of righteousness are all the result of a life lived in charity. In Jesus we see the perfection of these virtues, but not in a remote, otherworldly way. Jesus lived in the hurly-burly of life: the dusty roads, the pressing crowds, the surly challenges, and the endless demands. He does not tell us how to live from the serenity of a mountaintop; he shows us in a human life replete with blood, sweat, and tears. As the prophets were the voice of God, so Jesus is the life of God seen under human conditions.

But where do we begin? How do we heed such voices, follow the virtues of such a life? Let me make a suggestion. One spring at the annual meeting for the society of Episcopal college chaplains, I had the pleasure of walking around a restored Shaker village. In the large meeting room, we saw some of the Shaker dances and heard some of their hymns. One stayed in my mind. The words were, "Love is little, love is low, love will make your spirit grow." As you reflect on the words of the prophet Micah and the Beatitudes of our Lord, I suggest you build these virtues through the small and lowly dimensions of your life. From such beginnings, virtues grow. Our character is the product of daily thoughts, words, and actions. Justice begins as fair play and charity as a small act of kindness. Humility is to simply remember that we are of the earth, and to stay in right relationship with God. Each virtue begins as a word or act that we do with more than ourselves in mind.

Now to God, who has told us what is good through the prophet Micah and has shown us what is good in the person of Christ, let us give the requisite response of just, kind, and humble lives.

Chapter Seven

"Who Touched Me?"

Mark 5:22-24, 35b-43 | THE HEALING OF JAIRUS' DAUGH-
ter is a story of many dimensions, but
it is also a story that surrounds
another story. The other story is another healing miracle but it is
one that was not included in the lectionary. Yet it is intricately
woven into the story of the healing of Jairus' daughter. Just after
Jairus begged Jesus to come and heal his little girl, Jesus immediately changed whatever plans he had and went with the distraught
father. It is at this point that the story within the story begins.
Listen to what follows:

> And a large crowd followed him and pressed in on him. Now there
> was a woman who had been suffering from hemorrhages for twelve
> years. She had endured much under many physicians, and had spent
> all that she had; and she was no better, but rather grew worse. She had
> heard about Jesus, and came up behind him in the crowd and touched
> his cloak, for she said, "If I but touch his clothes, I will be made well."
> Immediately her hemorrhage stopped; and she felt in her body that
> she was healed of her disease. Immediately aware that power had gone
> forth from him, Jesus turned about in the crowd and said, "Who
> touched my clothes?" And his disciples said to him, "You see the crowd
> pressing in on you; how can you say, 'Who touched me?' " He looked
> all around to see who had done it. But the woman, knowing what had
> happened to her, came in fear and trembling, fell down before him,
> and told him the whole truth. He said to her, "Daughter, your faith

has made you well; go in peace, and be healed of your disease." (Mark 5:24*b*-34)

The Gospel continues; a message came from Jairus' house with news that his daughter had died. Jesus ignored the message and went on to the house. There the people had begun their mourning, and still Jesus persisted. He went in and took the child's hand and told her to get up. To the amazement of all, she did. And then Jesus asked them to give her something to eat.

Here we have two stories of the healing of women: one, a young child on the brink of womanhood, and the other, a woman who by her disease was ritually unclean and consequently an outcast in society. The first is a story of a child whom Jesus went to see. She had an advocate, namely her father, to intercede for her. Jesus' visit to her house was a public event and the crowd knew that Jesus was going there. In fact, the publicity was potentially scandalous for Jairus, a leader of the synagogue. His great love for his little girl led him to humble himself and risk his reputation as he begged the itinerant Jesus to heal his child.

In contrast, the woman with the hemorrhage had no one to intercede for her. Because she was ritually unclean, she had to act covertly. Under Jewish law, she should not have touched a man (Lev. 15:25), especially a holy man. Her approach to Jesus was daring and in secret. This makes her story unusual and particularly moving.

The stories have some interesting parallels: The woman with the issue of blood had been suffering as long as the little girl had been living. And Jairus' daughter was just at that age in Jewish society when a girl was recognized as a woman. Also, both women were designated as daughters. Jesus called the woman with the hemorrhage "Daughter," the only time he used such an address. But more than all else, both stories are stories of faith. In Jairus we see faith struggling to be born despite fear of loss and fear of ridicule. The woman with the hemorrhage dares to live the kind of faith Jairus is struggling to find.

She thought that all she needed to do was simply touch the garment of Jesus and she would be made well. In ancient times, beliefs in the curative powers of a healer's garments, handkerchief, even shadow, were common. Such things were viewed as extensions of the person. The woman wanted to touch Jesus, and the expression "at least his garments" marked the intensity of her desire. Her faith overrode any fear of making Jesus unclean.

Did you notice any curious aspects to this healing? Were you puzzled that the healing apparently took place before Jesus had knowledge of it? Did you wonder why he asked, "Who touched my garments?" and what he meant when he said he felt a power go forth? This story is unique in raising such questions, and the miracle can be understood in a variety of ways.

One possible interpretation comes from studies on healing. When healing takes place there is often a feeling like that of an electric current. Perhaps such a current is what Jesus experienced when the woman with the flow of blood drew forth his healing power by her need and her faith.

When Jesus said, "Your faith has made you well," he literally meant that. Jesus could certainly heal people of his own accord, but the faith of others apparently could draw upon his healing power and may even have been partially prerequisite for healing to occur.

Healing is a mystery that cannot be rationally understood. In this story there was an exchange of power or energy that preceded dialogue and had a compassion of its own. The subsequent dialogue formalized and reaffirmed the healing that had already taken place. Jesus' words to the woman reaffirmed his willingness to heal but asserted it was her faith that healed her. When he added, "Go in peace, and be healed of your disease," it was more than a dismissal. It was a reassurance that her disease was cured and would not return.

My mother has often quoted the actor Ethel Waters, who said, "You've got to pray with suction." The woman with the hemorrhage prayed "with suction," drawing healing and blessing from Jesus. Such determination and such "suction" puts her in the company of the Canaanite woman whose intelligence and ready wit changed Jesus' mind (Matt. 15:21-28), and of the persistent widow in Jesus' parable who finally persuaded the unjust judge to vindicate her (Luke 18:1-5).

All of us have private pain and, in a sense, all of us bleed. But sometimes the pain takes over and it is as if we are constantly bleeding. The story of the woman with the issue of blood tells us of release and healing after a long, long illness. She brings a message to those suffering chronic pain and long-term disease. At such times it is especially easy to feel far away from God, but she continued to seek to touch Jesus, despite the crowd of things that could have come between them.

The healing of Jairus' daughter tells of healing when all hope is gone. When Jesus said, "The child is not dead but sleeping," the crowd laughed at him. They were astonished at what they perceived as stubborn foolhardiness. Jesus kept asking Jairus to have faith in spite of the crowd and his own parental anxiety. And that is what Jesus asks of us: hope in the face of what seems utterly hopeless, and faith to move mountains.

The good news of these healing stories is threefold. First of all, when God in Christ walked among us, we see that God valued the feminine and sought to heal where it was ill or injured. Jesus valued women, young and old, rich and poor, socially acceptable and unacceptable. This is borne out in many Gospel stories, but these stories tell us that Jesus went out of his way to heal a little girl, and that he accepted and healed a woman who was ritually unclean.

Second, these stories, particularly the story of the woman with the issue of blood, tell us poignantly of the shame of disease, particularly diseases associated with the private parts of the body and with our sexuality. AIDS is the most recent in a long list of diseases that have brought shame as well as suffering. Many of our lives or those of our loved ones have been touched by such illnesses. Jesus' healing and loving acceptance of the woman with the hemorrhage offers dignity and hope for all who suffer shame as well as disease.

Last, these stories emphasize the importance of our faith. It is a crucial element in healing and wholeness whether that faith struggles to overcome fear and despair, as in the case of Jairus, or it is a faith that knows no boundaries, as in the case of the woman with the hemorrhage. This latter faith rushes on, trusting fully in a good and loving God who desires our restoration and our health. Jesus urges us to have such radical trust.

The story of the woman with the hemorrhage, the story within the story, the story that is not proclaimed in churches on Sunday mornings, tells us of a faith so strong that it drew out a blessing before it was consciously given. Then, when the blessing was consciously given, Jesus said, "Your faith has made you well." The story almost shouts that truth.

Chapter Eight

The Lord Is My Shepherd

John 10:11-16 | THE OTHER DAY I WAS WALKING OUR LABrador retriever when I saw a very small, dark squirrel cautiously coming across the street at an intersection. It was so small I wasn't sure the driver of the oncoming car could see it, so I gestured and the car stopped. The tiny squirrel then proceeded to follow me. I was taken aback. It seemed confused, and I did have a big black dog with me, but onward it came, undeterred. I was going to leave it, assuming it was young and its mother would find it, but the driver of the car (who had stopped to look at the tiny creature) told me he had three cats and knew the squirrel would not survive on the ground. Oddly, the squirrel was not afraid and came right to me, and curled up as if safe at last.

So I took it home and began calling the animal rescue services. It was after five in the evening and the offices were closed, but a voice message assured me that a volunteer would return my call before eight. When the call came, I learned that abandoned or orphaned baby squirrels will head for the first moving thing larger than they are, in hopes of finding warmth and security. I was advised to put the tiny squirrel in a large pocket so it could be close to me for warmth. Feeling somewhat marsupial, I did so until I was able to give the squirrel to a volunteer.

I mention this story because I believe it has bearing on our Gospel reading. While most of us who live in urban America have scarcely seen a sheep, much less a shepherd, this image from an earlier agrarian culture is oddly compelling, as well as comforting. The Twenty-third Psalm is *the* scripture most often read at the bedsides of the sick and dying as well as at funerals. I often request that students in my confirmation classes commit it to memory, not only for themselves, but so they can comfort others. Why do you suppose that such an image still has power to console us two millennia later?

I think the answer has something to do with the squirrel. His plight and behavior pointed out to me that it is often the creature in us that is aching, that longs for care, that wants someone to soothe our fears and give us warmth, security, and affection. In church we tend to focus a great deal on our spiritual dimension. But at such times we are decidedly more spiritual than Jesus. He lived in his body, healed other bodies, and was concerned about feeding people, both with loaves and fishes as well as with his body and blood. A shepherd is one who cares for the whole being of the sheep. The Twenty-third Psalm speaks of God's care for us in our entirety.

That little squirrel on the suburban cross streets was not unlike each of us. In moments of crisis, we find ourselves running toward we know not what, perhaps the open maw of a devouring creature or, with hope, a soft pocket where we will find security and warmth. The Good Shepherd, our Incarnate Lord, assures us that there is love for our animal selves in God who made us, not only in God's own image, but as mammals with the same needs for life as other mammals. At times we forget that when Christ took on our humanity, he also became a mammal, sharing with us (and many other creatures) development inside a mother's body, warm red blood, a four-chambered heart, and an instinct to care for the young.

Archbishop William Temple wrote, "It may safely be said that one ground for the hope of Christianity . . . lies in the fact that it is the most avowedly materialist of all the great religions. . . . Its own most central saying is 'The Word was made flesh.' "[1] God does not disdain the human body, nor our fellow creatures, nor the natural world. All of God's creation is beloved of God and under God's care.

In her book *Prayer, Stress, and Our Inner Wounds,* Flora Wuellner tells of a particularly compelling image of a shepherd which stayed with her from childhood. It is not the robed and peaceful person holding a small lamb with a flock at his feet that we often see depicted in stained-glass windows. Rather it is a tattered and bleeding person who had crawled down a steep cliff edge to rescue a lamb that had fallen. The lamb was injured and a bird of prey circled overhead. Wuellner writes, "I could not see the shepherd's face as he strained down to the sheep, but I could see the knotted muscles, the bleeding hands and arms gashed by thorns, the twisted garment torn in the steep descent."[2] She could see that the determined shepherd was paying a painful price to rescue the lamb, and that the lamb would be saved.

Who among us does not long for someone who would risk as much for us? Christ, in taking on our humanity, has already come to the rescue of each individual. But part of the Christian journey is to come to know Christ's love and faithfulness through our prayer and daily life. "In the Christian story God descends to re-ascend," wrote C. S. Lewis. "He comes down; down from the heights of absolute being into time and space, down into humanity; down further still, if embryologists are right, to recapitulate in the womb ancient and pre-human phases of life; down to the very roots and sea-bed of the Nature He had created. But He goes down to come up again and bring the whole ruined world up with Him."[3]

All of us, at times, feel like a frightened animal. Our Lord understands not only because he is the Good Shepherd, but because he is also the Lamb of God who suffered and died a very human and very creaturely death. He understands fear, pain, and despair.

All of us have a share of pain and suffering, and many of us will despair. Oscar Wilde knew despair and expressed it with these words:

> My heart is in some famine-murdered land
> . . . all good things have perished utterly,

But Wilde also knew the love of God and the promise of the Good Shepherd. He trusted that he would not suffer alone. His poem testifies to that trust as it concludes:

> . . . .
> peace, I shall behold, before the night,
> The feet of brass, the robe more white than flame,
> The wounded hands, the weary human face.[4]

What more could we ask for? Take heart and remember that you, too, in your darkest hour, will be shepherded by gentle hands, a very human face.

Chapter Nine

"Lord, . . . How Often . . . ?"

Matthew 18:21-35 IN THE EARLY PART OF THIS CENTURY, IN Gettysburg, Pennsylvania, a group of Civil War veterans who had fought in the famous battle there gathered for a reunion. As they stood about in the hotel lobby, a prosperous-looking businessman stopped suddenly before one of the veterans from an Ohio division and, in an accent tinged with the South, said, "Do you remember me?" When the old soldier said, "No," the Southerner recalled for him an evening in which a young, wounded Confederate soldier had been taken prisoner and was ill and in pain. A Union soldier had shared his food with him. The old soldier slowly began to remember and said, "But how did you recognize me after all these years?"

The Southerner replied, "I could never forget your face."

The poet William Blake wrote:

> For Mercy has a human heart,
> Pity a human face,
> And Love, the human form divine,
> And Peace, the human dress.[1]

That Union soldier was my great-grandfather, Jerome Holloway, and that story tells us something about mercy and forgiveness, the heart of our Gospel reading. Matthew tells the parable of the unmerciful, or unforgiving, servant. It occurs only in Matthew's

Gospel, and tells us that, as recipients of God's boundless forgiveness, we should not be miserly about forgiving others.

Forgiveness seems such a simple thing, yet it is often a complex process. Most of us have struggled at times with forgiveness, and some of us are wrestling with it now. The petty and hurtful remark, the betrayal of trust, the abrupt change in a friend's manner, the spouse who left after twenty-five years, the estranged child—there are so many things that befall us all; there is so much to forgive.

And so Peter, wanting to limit the task, asks Jesus, "Lord, if another member of the church sins against me, how often should I forgive? As many as seven times?" Jesus replies, "Not seven times, but I tell you, seventy-seven times." And as Peter contemplates the exhaustion of his reservoir of human kindness, and the mighty task ahead, Jesus tells the story of the unforgiving servant.

In this parable, the spotlight shifts from the plight of the wronged one to the boundless love of God, and we see that our forgiveness of others is but a drop compared to the ocean of wrongs that God has already forgiven us. Still, like the unmerciful servant, we easily forget, discount God's mercy toward us, and rush to the judgment of others.

I once heard a Benedictine, Brother David Steindl-Rast, speak about modern culture. He said we were a culture of "takers." We take showers, breaks, rides, vacations, classes, jobs, walks, spouses, exercise. Our language mirrors our materialism. One of our major difficulties, according to Brother David, is the ease and readiness with which we take *offense* and the tremendous tenacity we have when asked to let it go, to forgive.

Let us look for a moment at the dynamics of forgiveness. Jesus tells us in the parable that there is a debt involved. A person has been wronged, something taken from him or her. The one who offended owes an account of it. But a peculiar thing happens: the wronged person gains something because of the offense. He or she gains a moral edge over the other, in direct proportion to the size of the offense.

Forgiveness is difficult because it means giving up that moral edge, giving it back and once more being on equal footing with the one who has hurt us or offended us. It means reinstating him or her into the moral universe. Psychology teaches that if we do not reinstate those who have offended us, we lop off a part of our lives that they represent.

If we have been hurt very badly, forgiving may seem impossible. At times we feel as if our moral edge is the only shred of self we have left. We are afraid that if we let it go, we will be absorbed into an immoral chaos that threatens to undo us. There is risk of death in forgiveness, but there is also resurrection, for forgiveness beckons us into a new order where God is in control and will minister to our pain, and through us to the offender and the whole world.

Not long ago the *San Jose Mercury News* carried a story about a man named Ed Kramer. Another man, Josef Watkins, had run over Kramer and dragged him by car for a mile down an expressway. Kramer was in a coma for a month, lost his left arm and right leg and the sight in one eye. Doctors were amazed that he survived at all. At the trial, Watkins pleaded guilty to attempted second-degree murder and was given ten years in prison. As Watkins left the courtroom, Kramer reached out his remaining arm to shake his assailant's hand. "Hey, Joe," he said, "Good luck." I suspect that in that simple gesture, both men tasted paradise.[2]

Jesus says to forgive. That is probably the strongest theme of the New Testament. When we do not forgive, we postpone our own healing. Brother David said that to really forgive someone meant to assume the blame. For most of us, that's too much to ask. But consider the possibility that such a moral shift may occur without our saying or even knowing it when we do forgive.

Jesus tells us to forgive seventy-seven times. To actually forgive someone that often and not simply indulge a person means to be very creative. It may teach us to grow from reluctant appeasers into creative peacemakers.

Perhaps forgiveness is a capacity that is a gift. It may be that one reason we find it so difficult to forgive is that we get stuck in our works and the works of others and we want only to judge or be judged by them. We have forgotten the gift of grace, which enables us to put on the mind of Christ and empowers others to radically transform their lives.

Jesus seemed able to forgive people instantaneously. While Jesus willingly took on human nature with all the pain that flesh is heir to, he embodied the wideness of God's mercy in his capacity to forgive.

I have often thought that one measure of our spiritual growth is how long it takes us to forgive. To move from decades to seconds may take many of us a lifetime, and then some.

Jesus tells us to forgive again and again. But if we look closely at his parable, we are presented with a strange inconsistency: We are told to forgive as the king forgives; yet when the servant doesn't forgive, the king (or God) becomes angry and punitive. We want to learn about forgiveness but seem to meet head-on the wrath of God.

However, if we study the text closely, we will see that the king knows exactly what he is doing. The servant has had ample opportunity to learn. He had been forgiven a debt of ten thousand talents, comparable to ten million dollars today, and he has not forgiven his fellow servant the equivalent of a twenty-dollar debt. The king perceives that additional loving-kindness would not faze a person so hard-boiled. Sometimes love in the form of firm discipline is misinterpreted as cruelty. The unmerciful servant needed tough love and a rude awakening. He had to be forced to forgive. Sometimes so do we.

I began with a story of forgiveness and mercy that took place on a battlefield where the lines of friend and foe were clearly drawn and strongly supported, where it was easier and more socially acceptable to keep those battle lines drawn than to bridge them. But my great-grandfather bridged them and shared his food with an enemy.

We are familiar with another story of forgiveness and the sharing of food, but in that story, when we retell the story of the Last Supper and celebrate Holy Eucharist together, we hear how Jesus became food for us all. Jesus knew how to forgive immediately, and could even do so before an offense. You recall that Judas was at the Last Supper, and Jesus offered himself to Judas as well.

So when we struggle with forgiveness, let us remember that Jesus, who became human for our sake, will nourish us with himself and with the grace to forgive, even seventy-seven times.

Chapter Ten

The Abomination of Desolation

| Mark 13:14-27 | "I BLESS THE LORD WHO GIVES ME COUNSEL; in the night also my heart instructs me." In my judgment this verse from Psalm 16 alludes to |

the wisdom in our dreams. Psychologists say dreams can teach us much about ourselves if we will study them and learn their meaning. Each night we are transported to where veiled powers rule our lives. We enter a world where thinly disguised archetypal forces enact dramas that will influence what we do. Although it resembles our waking reality, this world is one in which anything is possible and everything is rich and strange. It is a realm easily forgotten in morning light and, if remembered, may strike us as bizarre and difficult to understand.

I mention this world of dreams because our Gospel account from Mark can be viewed as a kind of dream. It is a strange and troubling Gospel lesson because it darkly portends cataclysm, and because Jesus rarely uses such language. We are used to his pronouncements and parables, his straightforward speech and stories, but this is a different form of speech altogether. Jesus is using apocalyptic speech, and the passage from Mark is part of a section often called "the little apocalypse." Apocalyptic writing is like the dreams of a community in great stress.

Apocalyptic utterance and writing emerge in times of crisis, when the veil that normally covers the world of dreams and myths is torn away, allowing ancient archetypal forces to find their voice. These forces are always with us and are the wellsprings of prophecy, poetry, and art. But in times of great stress, they will emerge in bold and raw forms to enact perceived contemporary events on a cosmic scale.

While apocalypse is a strange form, we must not dismiss its power or influence, or even its truth. Albert Schweitzer wrote, "The late Jewish Messianic worldview is the crater from which burst forth the flame of the eternal religion of love."[1]

Not long ago I was discussing these scripture readings with a particularly astute student at Stanford University. His remark may speak for many of us. He said, "I wouldn't know the abomination of desolation if it bit me on the leg." This curious term that so perplexed the student is present in the readings from both Daniel and Mark. The word *abomination* is interesting in itself. We don't use it much these days, and if we do, it is usually as a rhetorical flourish. Only very conservative religious groups use it with any ethical seriousness. The word itself has two possible roots. One means that which goes against God's blessing, and the other means that which goes against the human. In the book of Daniel, written about two hundred years before Christ, the phrase refers to the altar of Zeus that was erected on Yahweh's own altar. This altar was considered such an abominable blasphemy that it caused the temple to be deserted, left desolate—hence the abomination of desolation.

Biblical scholars believe that the "abomination of desolation" mentioned in Mark refers to the Roman destruction of Jerusalem in A.D. 70. Such an interpretation seems likely when we remember that Mark wrote his Gospel around that time and published it after the fall of the city. Luke, writing later, spoke much more directly. He said, "When you see Jerusalem surrounded by armies, then know that its desolation has come near" (Luke 21:20). Mark may have been writing when a clear reference to Roman power was unadvisable. Hence, he falls back on the phrase that had become a standard reference in his community for the forces of evil, "the abomination of desolation." But he also included a broad hint, "let the reader understand," to alert the reader to his message: Christians are to stand fast. Mark was calling for hope and strength. In the end times, they must keep the faith—that is the essential message of all apocalyptic utterance, no matter how obscure and at times vindictive it seems. It is a valiant cry of faith and trust in God.

While perhaps the best example of apocalyptic writing is the Revelation to John, there are other valuable examples in Scripture. Apocalyptic literature sees the world as a cosmic battleground between good and evil. The outcome, which is already determined, is represented in vivid, mysterious images of the world's end and the beginning of a new age. The powerful sense of hope expressed in these writings centers on the figure of a new leader—a messiah. This new leader is often associated with a figure called the Son of Man—a cosmic embodiment of the people of Israel who would represent them before God. Jesus seemed comfortable applying this term to himself. It is interesting that when Jesus took on human nature, he took on the role of advocate and redeemer, and accepted many titles, from Rabbi to Messiah, from Son of Man to Son of God.

We don't have to stretch our understanding very much to see forms of apocalyptic expression around us today. Luke Skywalker and Darth Vader are engaged in an apocalyptic battle in the film epic, *Star Wars*. The Evil Empire is finally defeated and the Knights of the Jedi can continue to bring about the new world order. Apocalyptic ideas seem appropriate for troubled times like ours. In more optimistic eras an apocalyptic view of the world seems foreign, peculiar, and, in the end, irrelevant. But today, when fear of the future seems pervasive, when we are anxious about our ecological future, our political future, and our biological future, we may find that the strange symbols of apocalypse have meaning for us, and we begin to understand why its bold call to faith became Holy Writ. Earl Rovit wrote, "The metaphor of the apocalypse is our best model for viewing our contemporary human condition. It alone gives us a large and flexible mythic form that is grand enough to allow a full expression of our agonies and aspirations . . . responsive to the major cataclysms of twentieth-century life and death."[2]

Still, apocalyptic passages perplex many Christians. We do not know how to understand them. We see some well-intentioned churches and other movements gaining popularity by taking such biblical predictions literally. The mainline churches have taken a somewhat different tack, which is well expressed in words written earlier this century. A professor, corresponding to a graduate student who was about to write a thesis on apocalyptic literature, ventured these words: "I have serious counsel to give you. If you would have a long life and would see good days, keep mum on the subject . . . a subject which is highly dangerous in these days . . . a subject which the good and the great conspire to shun."[3]

It is no longer helpful to shun such writings, but is there a middle ground between shunning them and placards that read, "Prepare to meet your doom"? How can we understand apocalypse in the last decade of the twentieth century? Does it have meaning for our lives? I think that it does. First of all, it speaks to our anxieties about the future. When passenger airplanes explode in midair, and scientists report that sea life along the coast is dying, we realize that the future is not secure. When the Red River overflows its banks, increased numbers of species become endangered, and federal buildings are blown up in Oklahoma City, we can relate to fears of the final days. Few residents of California can fail to see the similarities between the first-century images of flight and the summer fires that periodically rage from the dried grasslands into residential hills. At such times, how eerily contemporary the admonition sounds: "The one on the housetop must not go down or enter the house to take anything away."

But more than historical catastrophes, these passages speak to us of the last things, of the end of the world. They attempt to answer the anxious questions: Toward what end are we heading? Who or what will have the final word? The answer is always the same. God is in charge. Trust God through hell and back. Difficult times are to be expected, but the ultimate victory belongs to God. The passage from Mark continues with these words:

> But in those days, after that suffering,
> the sun will be darkened,
> and the moon will not give its light,
> and the stars will be falling from heaven,
> and the powers in the heavens will be shaken.
> Then they will see "the Son of Man coming in clouds" with great power and glory. Then he will send out the angels, and gather his elect from the four winds, from the ends of the earth to the ends of heaven.

Those who have trusted in God will be saved. This is not to suggest that we simply trust and wait. Jesus taught us to live fully; to serve God and no other master; to turn to our neighbors with responsive love; and to trust that our acts of obedience, justice, and love will be part of God's plan.

The catechism of the Episcopal Church includes a question about our Christian hope. The answer reads, "The Christian hope is to live with confidence in newness and fullness of life, and to await the coming of Christ in glory, and the completion of God's purpose for the world." The catechism then asks what we mean by the coming of Christ in glory and the response is, "We mean that Christ will come, not in weakness but in power, and will make all things new."[4] So be it. Even if our knees are quaking, let us lend our voice to the ancient prayer and say our own, "Amen. Come, Lord Jesus."

Chapter Eleven

Creativity

Genesis 1–2:3

A YOUNG WOMAN ONCE TOOK A WALK IN THE woods and wrote these words about a tulip tree:

There's real power here. It is amazing that trees can turn gravel and bitter salts into these soft-lipped lobes, as if I were to bite down on a granite slab and start to swell, bud, and flower. Trees seem to do their feats so effortlessly. Every year a given tree creates absolutely from scratch ninety-nine percent of its living parts. Water lifting up tree trunks can climb one hundred and fifty feet an hour; in full summer a tree can, and does, heave a ton of water every day. A big elm in a single season might make as many as *six million* leaves, wholly intricate, without budging an inch; I couldn't make one. A tree stands there, accumulating deadwood, mute and rigid as an obelisk, but secretly it seethes; it splits, sucks, and stretches; it heaves up tons and hurls them out in a green, fringed fling. No person taps this free power; the dynamo in the tulip tree pumps out ever more tulip tree, and it runs on rain and air.[1]

"In the beginning . . . God created the heavens and the earth." I am pleased to say it is still here—precariously perhaps, but here—and this morning at dawn, it looked as dewy and fresh as if just from the word of God. The created, natural world is splendid, and in it we are refreshed and renewed.

Trinity Sunday is the one Sunday each year devoted to that mysterious dance of unity, the Trinity, in which we live and move and have our being. This day offers an opportunity to shed some light on one characteristic of that concept, namely the creative aspect of God. Of *Father, Son and Holy Spirit,* or *Creator, Redeemer, Sustainer,* it is the

Father, or Creator dimension, that brings forth creation from chaos. A newer formulation of the Trinity, *World-Maker, Pain-Bearer, Love-Giver,* clearly describes God's creative work.

Our First Lesson tells the story of creation. You may remember that there are two creation stories in Genesis, the story of Adam and Eve, and this one. This one is a later story and it is the story of creation par excellence. There are no other issues interwoven, such as sin and "the Fall." It is as straightforward as the poet James Weldon Johnson imagined:

> And God stepped out on space,
> And he looked around and said:
> I'm lonely—-
> I'll make me a world.[2]

We might take from this creation account an encouragement toward vegetarianism or a mandate for rest and relaxation after six days of work, but essentially its message is the record of creation. It almost follows our understanding of evolution in its order and development of the natural world.

From this story we have an image of God as creating, calling a world into being piece by piece, putting disorder into order and then affirming the goodness of it all. God doesn't make shoddy goods, God doesn't make confusion. God creates abundant life and says it is good. God is on the side of pattern and order, system and growing complexity, and hails it all as good.

And while we cannot create a world, or even a living leaf, we can participate in this dimension of God. We do so in our own creativity, for it is there that we touch something of the divine. In his book *The Courage to Create*, Rollo May discussed the creative process. Creation is bringing something new into being. It involves an encounter, an absorption, a sustained involvement, and a deep joy. Often it gathers input from unconscious realms of our being, and then something emerges, a new form or original expression. May writes, "The creative process is the expression of . . . passion for form. It is the struggle against disintegration, the struggle to bring into existence new kinds of being that give harmony and integration."[3]

We usually think of creation in terms of art; but it happens in many spheres of life, such as scientific discovery, invention, diplomacy, and child-rearing. Creativity can also happen in our life of faith. We tend to regard faith as something established and given, something we hold on to and sometimes lose. But couldn't it also be a dimension of life in which we use our imagination? It takes at least as much creative effort, energy, and intelligence to do good as to do evil, or nothing. Duke Ellington once said, "I merely took the energy it takes to pout and wrote some blues."[4]

Think for a moment of the creative process we undergo simply to apologize, to even see and admit we are wrong, much less do something about it. What an amazing feat and work of art to convert an average person into a Christlike nature. All that transformation—suspicion to trust, vindictiveness to forgiveness, pride to humility, doubt to faith—the list is endless and repetitive. Yet it happens. We all know it does. Maybe not as often as we would like, maybe not as close to home, but it happens. Someone once said that a saint is an artist without a craft. The life becomes the canvas, the music, or the poem.

In the life of faith, the tool of creativity is love. Love is both the means and the end of the creative process. When we love we are participating in the creative process of God. God did not create the world and then stop. God goes on creating and re-creating. The theologian Mary Daly asked, "Why indeed must 'God' be a noun? Why not a verb . . . the most active and dynamic of all?"[5]

We see the creativity of love most clearly in the Incarnation. "For God so loved the world that he gave his only Son . . . " (John 3:16). A colleague once remarked that we could almost expect Easter from a God—a grand reversal, a blinding sunrise—but Christmas? Christmas is so improbable, such an amazing rough and tumble story, such a scandalous, crazy plan. To enter our world as a poor human child—how did God ever imagine such an astonishing strategy?

The Creator God made the world, and that making was and is an act of love. If we can learn to love, we also become creators of the reign of God. And if we learn to flow out in love to others and to the natural world, we will come to know intimately the creative dimension of God that was Father to Jesus Christ.

A seventeenth-century English mystic wrote:

You never enjoy the world aright, till the sea itself flows in your veins, till you are clothed with the heavens, and crowned with the stars, and perceive yourself to be the sole heir of the whole world, and more than so, because others are in it who are every one sole heirs as well as you. Till you can sing and rejoice and delight in God, as misers do in gold, and Kings in sceptres, you never enjoy the world.[6]

May we all know the joy of being both created and creator, lover and beloved.

Chapter Twelve

"Yes, Lord, Yet . . . "

Matthew 15:21-28

EXCLUSION HURTS. BEING A STRANGER, being left out, hurts. The memory of rejection is in most of our histories. Today's Gospel tells of Jesus' encounter with a stranger, a foreign woman who asks for his help. Jesus clearly sees his ministry and mission as serving his own people, the Jews. He has come to the district of Tyre and Sidon, leaving Jerusalem and the continuous questioning of the scribes and Pharisees. According to Matthew's chronology, Jesus has just had the most serious confrontation with the organized Jewish leaders, calling them hypocrites who uphold tradition rather than the Word of God. His time in Tyre and Sidon could be understood as time apart to meditate, to regroup, to rest before reentering the arena.

It is in this context that the Canaanite, or Syrophoenician, woman makes her appearance. She is not a Jew, she is a pagan, yet she addresses Jesus with the Jewish acclamation, "Son of David." She asks him to have mercy on her, for her daughter is tormented by a demon. Her daughter is divided and broken, and the woman begs for the psychological health of her child. Jesus' first response is silence. Then the disciples ask Jesus to send her away because she is following them and has become an annoyance. Jesus tells her that he was sent only for the lost sheep of the house of Israel. But the woman implores, kneels before Jesus, and asks again for help. To this plea Jesus answers, "It is not fair to take the children's food and throw it to the dogs."

What happens next makes this story a pivotal one in the Gospels. The woman's response is masterful. She takes Jesus' metaphor and turns it to her own advantage. "Yes, Lord, yet even the dogs eat the crumbs that fall from their masters' table." Jesus is so impressed by her quick wit and easy humility that he changes his mind. He reassesses the situation and decides to do what she asks.

It is important to note that this encounter marks a change of direction in Jesus' ministry as well, moving him into the Gentile world, the larger world beyond the confines of the Jewish people. The Gospel of Matthew proceeds from this point to the feeding of the four thousand on a mountainside near the shore of the Sea of Galilee, and we may legitimately presume the eastern shore, which would place Jesus' nourishment of the multitude in Gentile lands. This persistent and wise Canaanite woman opened the door to the rest of the world.

Now, what does this mean for us? The Canaanite woman was a stranger, a woman outside the covenant. Our human nature (as well as the legitimate caveats of childhood) seems to make most of us ill at ease with strangers, but part of our growth into the full stature of Christ is the acceptance of what may at first seem strange and unfamiliar to us. We learn much from the stranger; we learn about our world and about ourselves. We learn to stretch our understanding and, if we persist, we learn to accept the undesirable, frightening, and strange parts of ourselves. If we are to be whole, healed, merciful people, our task must be to exclude no one. All are part of the human family. All are part of us.

This story also speaks to us about distractions and interruptions. As you recall, the Canaanite woman had become an irritation, a bother. The disciples wanted her to go away. Perhaps Jesus wished to be rid of her, too. He and the disciples had much to think about, much to do, and little time.

There is probably not one of us who cannot understand the tremendous need to be undisturbed. Whether it's work to be done, rest to be gained, prayer or simply quiet we need, interruptions can become irritating and exhausting. It seems at times that one's whole day, or week, or even life is deferred while we answer other people's agendas. C. S. Lewis once said that he so often felt distracted from his real work that he began to wonder if perhaps the distractions were the real work that God intended. He wrote, "What we call hindrances are really the raw material of the spiritual life. As if the fire should call the coal a hindrance. One can imagine a little young fire, which had been getting on nicely with the sticks and paper, regarding it as a mere cruelty when the big lumps were put on: never dreaming what a huge steady glow, how far surpassing its present crackling infancy, the Tender of the fire designed it when he stoked it."[2]

If we allow the possibility, and can get beyond the sense of hindrance, the supposed disturbance to our search for God might become the means to a deeper faith. In the case of the Canaanite woman, her intrusion caused a major revision. Suddenly a foreign woman was moved from the periphery of concerns to a central place in the household of faith.

Finally, this Gospel lesson tells us something of our interaction with God. When Jesus says to the Canaanite woman, "It is not fair to take the children's food and throw it to the dogs," he was likening the Jews to children and the Gentiles to dogs. Many a Gentile would have been offended. But the Canaanite woman did not take offense, nor did she react defensively. In effect, she rolled with the punch and she took the metaphor even further, skillfully turning the image of dog from a wild beast by a garbage heap to the friendly beast beneath the family table. She made herself, by hook and by crook, part of the family. "Yes, Lord, yet even the dogs eat the crumbs that fall from their masters' table."

She demonstrated that she was not only capable of humility but that she was also a mind and a spirit to be reckoned with. Jesus was so impressed by her that he reversed his decision. In the Gospel according to Mark, Jesus says, *"For saying that,* you may go—the demon has left your daughter."[3] With this passage, we see more clearly Jesus' response to her carefully wrought answer.

Her insistence reminds me of an event that took place more than twenty years ago in Philadelphia. The Episcopal Church had decided that women could not be ordained as priests or consecrated as bishops. Eleven women deacons said, in effect, "Yes, Lord, yet . . . tradition must be enlarged to contain a larger truth," and they were ordained to the all-male priesthood of the church. The ordinations were considered irregular and were felt by some to be an annoyance and an irritating problem. Regardless of the controversy, however, something had changed, once and forever. Years later the church would vote to change the rules, but we will never know where history would have gone without that event in Philadelphia. Eleven insistent women set change in motion, making the call to priesthood possible for their sisters throughout the Anglican communion, and ultimately opening the door to the episcopacy for them as well.

In the early part of this century, Edwin Markham wrote:

> He drew a circle that shut me out—
> Heretic, rebel, a thing to flout.
> But Love and I had the wit to win:
> We drew a circle that took him in![4]

The Canaanite woman shows us how to overcome exclusion even of the highest order. She used her mind and wit in the service of her love for her daughter. She drew a larger circle, showed a broader perspective, and love was the motivating force. When we use our intellectual skills and capacity to their fullest extent in our relationship with God, God responds to us in new and surprising ways.

But that's not all; this story also tells us about "chutzpah" and persistence as well as the use of our minds. It tells us about a woman who heard a clear "no" from God but would not take "no" for an answer. She demanded that her daughter be made whole, free from torment. She was the conversational equivalent of Jacob, who would not let go until he had wrested a blessing from his winged assailant. She was as tenacious as Abraham bargaining with God for the lives in Sodom and Gomorrah. And, like her predecessors, she was successful. When we persist with the full strength of our God-given minds, God knows it is a force to be reckoned with.

We have seen in this Gospel a dialogue charged with energy, creativity, and change. Jesus summarized the law as loving God with all your heart, with all your soul, and with all your *mind*.[5] The Canaanite woman did just that. Let us resolve to do the same.

Chapter Thirteen

The Body of Christ

| Matthew 25:31-46 |

THE BODY OF CHRIST. AS CHRISTIANS, we often hear this phrase, and many of us have some understanding of what it means. But I would like to explore the phrase and see if we can come to understand it in some new ways. Let's assume we are hearing it for the first time. Our initial impression would be that it refers to a body. Jesus, the Christ, had a body. He was probably dark, with dark hair and eyes. We can imagine him about medium height. He was a man and, using the calendar created in his honor, a first-century Jew. He probably did not look much like the Jesus depicted in many classic European paintings. It is very unlikely that he was a blue-eyed blond. We can imagine him a young man; we know he didn't live beyond his early thirties.

We know that Jesus did physical things that most human bodies do. He was born and grew up. He ate and drank, walked and slept, sought shelter and wore clothes, touched people and socialized. We also know that he wept, sought companionship, felt afraid, suffered, bled, and died. That is an overview of his bodily life. If you were to describe the life of your own body, you would no doubt have a much more detailed story, but this is just an overview. And this is where the Body of Christ begins, in the body of Jesus. It is important that we begin here.

In theological parlance we speak of the Incarnation, which means that God became human. It is a word that comes from the Latin and means "to be made flesh." It has the same roots as *carnal* and *carnage*.

It refers to flesh and blood, muscle and bone. But the Body of

Christ came to mean more than just the body of Jesus. The concept expanded as the church's understanding of Jesus grew.

Christ means "the anointed one" or "messiah" in Greek. The Christ was the longing of the Jewish people, who expected another leader like King David. When the term *Christ* came to be applied to Jesus and the early church began to realize that Jesus was "the Word made flesh," the body of Jesus gained an entirely new significance.

This was further increased by Paul, who wrote letters to develop and encourage the first Christian communities. He came to see that the Body of Christ was much larger than the physical body of Jesus. In Paul's First Letter to the Christians at Corinth, he said, "For as in Adam all die, so also in Christ shall all be made alive. . . . The last enemy to be destroyed is death" (1 Cor. 15:22-26 RSV).

It became understood among Christians that the Body of Christ lives in the followers of Jesus and in the sacrament of the Holy Eucharist. In that ritual we proclaim, as Jesus did, that bread becomes his body and wine becomes his blood. Consequently, we who partake become part of the mystical Body of Christ, which includes the living and the dead. The faithful, or the church, now has become the Body of Christ in the world.

Our Gospel story is a story that contains the essence of our faith. Jesus tells a story about the end times. He shows us the final day of judgment and reckoning. And essentially he talks about bodies. He commends those who cared for the bodies of others: those who fed, clothed, housed, and visited those in need. He identifies the needy bodies with God's body. Likewise, he chastises those who did not attend to the bodies of the needy, and reminds them that they ignored God's presence among them by their actions.

This is the only detailed description of the last judgment that is given in the Gospels. While it is a parable, it is also prophecy. Jesus expresses the ethical law of Judaism as well as the Christian law of love. In it the Son of Man, which was a name Jesus applied to himself, judges the nations, separating the righteous or just from the un-righteous or unjust.

The Son of Man is an apocalyptic term. It was first used by the prophets and initially meant one who stood for all, as in one person standing for all humanity. Over time, it came to mean a heavenly being that looks like a person. Leo Baeck points out that, originally, people looked to the Son of Man horizontally as in the hope for a king of David's line; later, the connection became vertical. He says,

"There the expected one, the object of longing, is a scion of the house of David who will fulfill history; here he has become the supernatural being who descends from the heavenly heights to end history."[1]

The Son of Man will separate the just from the unjust. The separation is as clear as the separation of Syrian sheep and goats, which are white and black respectively. The criterion is sixfold and the story repeats it four times. It is simple but direct, and clearly stated. The righteous, or just, are those who fed the hungry, gave drink to the thirsty, welcomed the stranger, clothed the naked, visited the sick, and showed concern for prisoners. The unrighteous, or unjust, are those who did not.

Robert McAfee Brown points out, "What really counts before God is not what we thought. The important things are not (a) regular church attendance, (b) praying daily, (c) knowing the Apostles' Creed, (d) tithing, or even (e) confessing Jesus Christ as Lord and Savior. Admirable though such characteristics of Christian living may be, they do not even rate a passing nod in Jesus' assessment. All that counts in Jesus' assessment is—helping those in need."[2]

The six criteria that Jesus gives all deal with bodies. Most of us have known hunger, thirst, isolation, cold, illness, or confinement, to greater or lesser degrees. Jesus asks us to extend our understanding to identify with the suffering of others and makes it clear that he identifies with them to the extent that what happens to them, happens to him. Many of us have seen pictures of the hungry. They are not the usual photos in our age of media hype. But as famine is usually taking place somewhere in our world, we see the faces of hunger. However, lest we distance ourselves because the needy seem so far away, all we need to do is look at the homeless person pushing a shopping cart on our suburban streets.

We are used to seeing pictures of robust athletes, beautiful movie stars, familiar political leaders. But the images of the hungry that flash across our screen—the prematurely aged mother, the shriveled, stick-legged child, the old man picking the dust for seeds—these are different because they are not identified except for their condition. They have no names. They are just bodies.

Even before Jesus spoke of his body being given in the Holy Eucharist, he had begun to understand that his body was meant to extend to others. In this Gospel story, the body of the Son of Man, the body of Jesus, the Body of Christ is stretched to embrace and become the bodies of those who are suffering. He gives them his name.

Robert McAfee Brown says there is a prayer that some of us unconsciously pray. It goes, "Our Father who art in heaven . . . stay there."[3] It is easier to cope with a God who is far away, removed from our already too busy lives. We would rather God stay enthroned up on some distant star rather than muck about in our world. But God in Jesus did not do that. The Word became flesh. And it became flesh that would not be confined, limited to one body in one place. It is flesh that insists on being among us.

Both the unrighteous and the righteous were perplexed in this parable. Neither had seen the Lord. Yet one group had seen themselves in the others and responded with love and fellow feeling. The other group had seen only strangeness or wrongness—racially, economically, or politically—and so justified their lovelessness and lack of care. Perhaps they even viewed Jesus as the remote patron of their lack of compassion.

As voters, it is important to know that the judgment this Gospel pronounces is not a privatized one. The Gospel story is not about individuals so much as it is about groups. The Son of Man judges the "nations," not individual people. Charles Peguy once said that everything begins in mysticism and ends in politics.[4] This message from Christ tells us that our collective efforts matter. Where our tax dollars go, where our energies go, all of this has to do with our immortal souls.

And so it may be that the ultimate goal of the Body of Christ is to move into the body politic. This is not to suggest that we make Christianity the religion of the state. What it does suggest is that we suffuse our collective life with justice and make the six criteria of the judgment of the Son of Man a means whereby we evaluate our national achievement, as well as our personal commitment.

If you have ever experienced a newborn crying insistently, you know the urgency of need. Our own bodies signal us with pain that is immediate and insistent. If we could take others' pain as seriously as our own, we would begin to infuse the body politic with the immortal Body of Christ.

Jesus urges us to respond to the hurts of the world. He does not ask us to do so out of pity or noblesse oblige, nor does he suggest that we do so at a distance to keep ourselves from the downward pull of the disinherited. He asks us to respond to them as to himself among us, as Christ among us, as the sacrament, the Eucharist we share. For Jesus is there; he is there squatting in the dust: a tiny child, an anguished mother, a homeless veteran. His bond with the hungry, the sick, the homeless, is not remote. He has told us, "Just as you did it to one of the least of these who are members of my family, you did it to me." "Inasmuch," he said, "likewise." He is there. The bond is like that of a parent to a child, or even closer. It is love's own identity.

So much of Christian life is finding Christ anew, finding points of meeting that we had hitherto overlooked. Jesus placed himself squarely in the commonplace, in food and drink, but also in those places that would stretch us, force us to grow in compassion. Jesus says he is there in those forced to walk the way of the cross. His is the name we are to give to the stranger, the hungry, the bodies and faces without names. Can we see him? Will we meet him there?

I suppose each of us can recall walking past him, not in a state of recognition, but in fear, even contempt, disgust. We have said in our actions, "I do not know the man." Jim Forest of the Orthodox Peace Fellowship writes, "If I cannot find the face of Jesus in the face of those who are my enemies, if I cannot find him in the unbeautiful, if I cannot find him in those who have the 'wrong ideas,' if I cannot find him in the poor and defeated, how will I find him in the bread and wine . . . ?"[5]

At some point, there will be a judgment on us and our compassion. Did we learn to love? Did we learn to share? Did our actions serve the justice of God? During Holy Communion you take into your body "the Body of Christ, the Bread of Heaven." As you are strengthened and renewed in that communion, remember these words of Teresa of Avila:

> Christ has
> No body now on earth but yours;
> No hands but yours;
> No feet but yours;
> Yours are the eyes
> Through which is to look out
> Christ's compassion to the world;
> Yours are the feet
> With which he is to go about
> Doing good;
> Yours are the hands
> With which he is to bless now.[6]

Chapter Fourteen

"Blessed Is the One"

Matthew 21:1-11;
26:36-27:66

"BLESSED IS THE ONE WHO COMES IN the name of the Lord." This is one of the most poignant phrases of Holy Week, one that we repeat when we remember Jesus' moment of entry into Jerusalem. It was said by the crowds at the time, quoting Psalm 118. It was as if the people of Jerusalem briefly understood who this person was, this man entering their city on a donkey as they scattered palm fronds on the road before him. The Jews had expected and hoped for a new king, a warrior who would release them from Rome, their most recent oppressor. Such a person would most likely enter the city on a stallion accompanied by a multitude of soldiers. But this day, it is as if they got a glimpse of their real oppressor, the sins that separated them from God and from one another; and the people understood that Jesus was the one who could set them free.

"Blessed is the one who comes in the name of the Lord." We repeat this phrase in our Eucharist. We say it at the end of the Sanctus when we sing, "Holy, Holy, Holy Lord, God of power and might." Jesus came into Jerusalem without the customary trappings of power. He came in the plain manner of humility and was received for just a moment into the hearts and consciousness of his people. As we have seen, that moment changed all too soon; and Jesus was met with betrayal, denial, humiliation, and mockery, which all but erased the moment of recognition. But not quite. For the glimpse would return as astonished vision and finally as new and revolutionary understanding about the human condition.

"Blessed is the one who comes in the name of the Lord." In the Gospel of Matthew, between the entry into Jerusalem and the account of the Passion, Jesus laments over Jerusalem with these words, "Jerusalem, Jerusalem, the city that kills the prophets and stones those who are sent to it! How often have I desired to gather your children together as a hen gathers her brood under her wings, and you were not willing! See, your house is left to you, desolate. For I tell you, you will not see me again until you say, 'Blessed is the one who comes in the name of the Lord' " (Matt. 23:37-39). It had not been long since the death of John the Baptist, and Jesus understood that he stood in the line of prophets whose very words unleash fury and violence in those who do not worship the living God.

"Blessed is the one who comes in the name of the Lord." This is one beatitude that Jesus asks his followers to repeat. What exactly does it mean? "Blessed is" has been translated as "Happy is." It means that we receive and bless those whom God sends into our lives. Such people are to be made welcome, and we are to understand that they are enacting God's will among us. But it is often difficult to tell who it is that comes in the name of the Lord. That is where prayer and discernment are required. For all of us see through a glass darkly, and sometimes prophets and others who "come in the name of the Lord" aren't readily apparent. Some who claim to "come in the name of the Lord" may be wolves in sheep's clothing. And those who do come in God's name do not necessarily make us feel good about ourselves. In fact, they can be most unsettling. Remember John the Baptist addressing members of his congregation as "You brood of vipers" (Matt. 3:7). It is doubtful that many in that group responded, "Blessed is the one who comes in the name of the Lord."

In Paul's Letter to the Philippians, we hear beautiful words explaining why Jesus most clearly came "in the name of the Lord." Paul says, "Though he was in the form of God, did not count equality with God a thing to be grasped, but emptied himself, taking the form of a servant" (Phil. 2:6-7 RSV). The word *form* as Paul is using it does not mean outward shape, but rather inner essence. Though Jesus was God, he came as one of us, "in the name of the Lord." This passage is an early church song, celebrating the impetus of love in the mystery of the Incarnation. The words of this ancient hymn speak of Christ having the same nature as God and willingly taking on our human nature to fully comprehend the human condition.

"Blessed is the one who comes in the name of the Lord." Our scriptural account of the passion is one of blessing withheld. Jesus was given betrayal, denial, and curse instead of blessing. But woven into the story we see that light still pierced the darkness. Pilate's wife heard God speak in a dream and tried in vain to stop the wheels of history. The Roman centurion and those with him who had observed the passion of the crucifixion came to the realization, "Truly this was the Son of God" (Matt. 27:54 RSV). And Joseph of Arimathea, despite the obvious personal risks, stepped forward as a disciple to ask Pilate for the body of Jesus.

"Blessed is the one who comes in the name of the Lord." During Holy Week, I ask you to walk the way of the cross with these words on your lips. He who came in the name of God found that to do so was to walk a difficult and passionate path. His story is like no other; but we, as his followers, at times find ourselves on that hard, well-trodden road. It is our opportunity and privilege to enter deeply into that journey, to follow Christ through all the pain that human life can give, to feel his grief and loss, fear and passion, and to find in the midst of it his unbreakable blessing. And it is finally our call to allow God to transform our lives so that others can glimpse in us the fruits of God's love and learn to say with us, "Blessed is the one who comes in the name of the Lord."

Chapter Fifteen

God Forsaken

MOST OF US HAVE HAD AT LEAST ONE | Matthew 27:45-56 | prayer unanswered. It is a devastating realization when the desire of our heart is apparently unheard. In studying the efficacy of prayer, C. S. Lewis says that most answered prayers come early in our Christian journey. As we progress, answered prayers tend to be rarer. He points out that the refusals are not only more frequent but more unmistakable.[1] Clearly Christ's words on the cross before his tortured death are words of unanswered prayer. "Eloi, Eloi, lama sabachthani?" he cried out, using the words of the Twenty-second Psalm. "My God, my God, why have you forsaken me?" According to the evangelists Matthew and Mark, these were the last words of Jesus before he uttered one last cry and breathed his last.

Is it possible that Jesus' passion ended here, on this note of forsakenness and anguish? Perhaps there was not resignation and commendation such as Luke records with Jesus' words, "Father, into your hands I commend my spirit" (Luke 23:46). Perhaps there was not a sense of completion as we find in the Gospel of John when Jesus pronounces, "It is finished" (19:30). What if this is where the passion of our Lord concluded, with this, a cry of anguish, longing, need, and helplessness? This is the most passionate cry in all of Scripture.

And the cry itself provokes our questions. If Jesus was the Incarnate Lord, why was he forsaken? Was he not the one who made the moon and the stars? How could such a being, who was in fact All Being, be reduced to this? Had he forsaken himself? Was it all a sham? Did we have it all wrong? This is clearly a puzzle, but it is one that can be comprehended, and the answer will take us to the depths of God's love.

Through the teachings of Jesus and the gift of the Spirit, we have come to understand God as Trinity. The three persons of the Trinity are selfless, pure relations. Each of them is in constant relationship with the others. Such an understanding helps us as we are gathered here commemorating that the Lord of Life hung on a cross, suffering his forsakenness by that which had sustained him. It was out of love that Jesus took on the pain of being human to the point of taking Godlessness upon himself. The Swiss theologian Hans Urs von Balthasar says of this, "The crucified Jesus suffers . . . our interior estrangement from God and our experience of God's darkness."[2] Jesus let go of his intimacy with the love that moves the sun and the stars to bear all the estrangement that human beings in their lack of love can suffer. God experienced the absence of God.

And if we wonder why, the answer again is one of love. It is a love difficult to comprehend because it is beyond most human loving. But Christianity is the great school of love, and this is one of its central lessons. The British theologian John Saward says that Jesus "suffers an abandonment infinitely more wounding than that of sinners, one that somehow embraces theirs, bringing light into the midnight of their anguish, placing pierced hands of love beneath their fall."[3]

We often understand God as the Creator, who is benevolent, glorious, comforting. Such a God is the ground of our being, the source of human good, the ultimate reality. We can intellectually assent to such a God and worship the transcendent glory. The mind naturally gravitates toward such undifferentiated monotheism. Similarly, we understand Jesus as the gentle prophet/poet who spoke the truth, healed others, and was unjustly tortured and killed. We can love Jesus as one of us and feel outrage at his death. But what happens when we mix the two, as the Doctrine of the Incarnation does? Rosemary Haughton, another British theologian, writes: " 'Incarnation' is a word to which most people find it hard to give a meaning. It violates, as a concept, our sense of divine and human decency, it crosses a barrier which we require, for our mental and psychological comfort, to be impermeable."[4]

What happens when we say that God loves so passionately that God became human in the person of Jesus? What happens when we say that Jesus lived love so fully that he has to be God? It boggles the mind. This is outrageous. It is either absolute absurdity or absolute truth. Or, perhaps, both. Tertullian once said, "It is by all means to be believed, because it is absurd."[5]

But the innocent suffering we commemorate is still there, and something in us cries out at the huge injustice. Who can we blame? Can't we blame all-powerful God? And the answer is sorrowfully simple: No. God gave up power willingly in this moment. The blame must fall on human sin, those voices so much like our own that cried out betrayal, crucifixion, denial. George Herbert says of the agony Christ suffered:

> Sin is that press and vice, which forceth pain
> To hunt his cruel food through ev'ry vein.[6]

As we remember the last words of Jesus, we come ultimately to silence: the silence of Jesus and the silence of God. We hear the silence of the Incarnate Word, the Word made flesh that dwelt among us. We hear also the silence of unanswered prayer, the stillness that met our Lord's anguished request. And we come to our own silence, the silence of our own complicity and lack of love.

This is the moment when God was forsaken. This is the place of Godforsakenness, when there is no healing word, only silence. This is the time of human despair. This is the place of the absence of God. But even here our Lord will find us. It is not uncharted territory. It has been mapped, located, hallowed. Even Godforsakenness can be a holy and hopeful place because it has been known in its anguish by the person and presence of abiding Love.

Chapter Sixteen

Disbelief for Joy

Luke 24:36b-43

WHEN ASKED IF HE BELIEVED IN AN AF-
terlife, Woody Allen replied, "Yes, but I'm
afraid no one will tell me where it's being
held." All of us wonder just what will happen to us when we die. What
has happened to our loved ones who have already died? Like the
comedian, we have a vague fear of being left without all the necessary
information.

Several years ago, when I served as a parish priest, the retired
former rector of the parish, who had remained in the church and
worshiped there for many years, died. Shortly after the funeral, I had
a dream in which he visited me. He gave me a book and asked me to
take it to his wife, Helen, and tell her that everything would be all
right. I awakened and decided that I would call on his widow. I did
and told her of my dream. Of course I did not have the actual book
to give her, but I did have the comforting words that I shared. Helen
was reassured by the message I conveyed, and thankful that I had
come. I did not know the title of the book I was given in the dream,
but I suspect it was the Bible, which tells us the good news of Christ
overcoming death.

Just what is our Christian understanding of death? A common
response to the question of what happens when we die is an assured
belief in the immortality of the soul. Such a belief is comforting and
seems to be validated by contemporary out-of-the-body accounts of
those who have had near-death experiences. However, this is not our
Christian understanding. It is actually a Greek philosophical idea
that found its way into our culture and our churches and so has
remained. This idea holds that when the body dies, the soul is at last

82

released and goes on to eternal life. Our Christian faith teaches us, from Genesis, that body and soul are one. The Spirit of God breathes into a body, and that body becomes a living soul.

If we assume that when the body dies, the soul does not, as the ancient Greeks believed, the body is viewed as a prison house, excess baggage, something even gross and embarrassing. We see the effects of the separation of body and soul in many aspects of contemporary culture. The body is seen as imperfect baggage holding back the perfect soul. Consequences, from facelifts and body tucks to surgical sculpting, result from an attempt to curb the body and make it conform to the misguided ideal of the soul. The Swiss scholar Oscar Cullmann contrasted the death of Socrates with the death of Jesus. In the *Phaedo*, Plato described the serene death of Socrates, portraying him as willingly drinking the hemlock as if he simply shed his outer garment and peacefully flowed into eternity. Jesus, on the other hand, was agitated and fearful, asked his disciples to stay with him, and then died in agony and despair. He died this way because he truly died; all that he was went into death because it was only by dying that he could enter death's domain and then overcome it.[1]

In Christian doctrine we believe in the resurrection of the body. It is stated in all of the major creeds. This belief began with the resurrection of Jesus, but such life is the Christian hope for us all. We don't just have a body, we are a body; and when we die, all of us goes. Our Jewish heritage boldly sings praises in the Song of Songs of the glory of the body. Jesus enjoyed the life of his body so much that he was accused of being a glutton and a drunk. When his friend Lazarus died, Jesus did not speak of the soul's happy escape. Rather, he wept. Death was real. The whole person, the sum of his parts, was gone. And death came into the world because of sin: "The wages of sin is death" (Rom. 6:23). This equation began in Genesis. It is to this scheme of events that Jesus came. To alter it was the reason he set his face toward Jerusalem. And from his self-giving love a new divine act of creation emerged, and the man who was dead became the man who lives.

In the Gospel reading from Luke, we hear of one of the resurrection appearances of Jesus. He suddenly appears in the room as the disciples have been discussing him. They are frightened and afraid that they are seeing a ghost. Jesus addresses their fears and invites them to touch his body and to look carefully at him. They were doubtful because of their great joy, and then Jesus asked them if they had anything to eat. It is such a casual and comfortable request, one we would ask family or our closest friends. And they gave him a piece of fish, which he ate before them. This is an interesting detail, and one that emphasizes the corporeal, just as his sudden appearance in the room, his moving through walls and doors, emphasizes the spiritual dimension of his resurrected body. Then Jesus spoke to them and taught them. He opened their minds so they would at last understand what he had tried to tell them before. Then he commissioned them to preach to all nations in his name.

The Gospel accounts of Jesus after the Resurrection are stories full of wonder and contradiction. In them we can find some common threads. For example, in several instances Jesus was not recognized, then became known through the breaking of bread or by showing his wounds. He would also appear suddenly among the disciples, as in our Gospel reading, and then he would do something very physical, such as eat or prepare a meal. From these accounts it is clear that the disciples were confused, overwhelmed, and so overjoyed that they doubted what was happening. It is also clear that the resurrection body of Jesus had new properties as well as some very familiar ones. The resurrection body is a new creation of the divine will, but it bears the imprints of the suffering and sacrifice that we have done for love while we have lived on earth. Someone once said that the things we take with us when we die are the things we have given to the poor. It may also be that we will be recognized after death by the scars of our moments of self-giving love.

There is wide divergence among biblical scholars and people of faith concerning the resurrection of Jesus. There are those more orthodox who believe in the objective evidence as presented in the Gospel accounts; and there are also, within the household of faith, those who believe that something happened of tremendous significance, but they can only place that event within the disciples' subjective experience. All agree, and even agnostics and atheists must concur, that something so extraordinary happened that the measuring of time since has been dated from the life of Jesus.

Despite differing opinions on the actual resurrection of our Lord, Christian doctrine still maintains the resurrection of the body as the hope for us all after we die. The statement of belief in the creeds adheres to: "The forgiveness of sins, the resurrection of the body, and the life everlasting," as we say in the Apostles' Creed. The appearance of Jesus to his disciples showed them the "first fruits" of what was to come. No doubt they disbelieved for joy. After dreading and yet realistically expecting death all your life, would you not disbelieve such a joyous reversal? G. K. Chesterton once wrote, "Joy, which was the small publicity of the pagan, is the gigantic secret of the Christian."[2] Unfortunately, in many cases it has remained secret. Our missionary zeal has often done more to propound belief than to convey joy. But joy is there. This body, at least some recognizable facsimile thereof, is bound for glory, and the same can be said for each of us. That is cause for joy.

However, we are aware that dead bodies appear to remain in the grave. This seems problematic in the light of Christian hope. It is here that we come to understand why the Greek idea of the immortality of the soul offered a solution to the dilemma and so crept into Christian thinking. Christian understanding of what happens when we die is basically a hope of resurrection, but again there is a divergence of understanding within the household of faith. To be clear, we must speak of eschatology, or the last things. The New Testament, taken as a whole, was dominated by the thought that a new age was at hand. This new age would be ushered in by a final judgment in which the dead would be raised.

In the intervening centuries, the immediacy of that expectation has had to change. We have come to see the new age, the second coming of Christ, as always at hand, as both here and coming. Consequently, our understanding of the resurrection of the dead has changed to accommodate our eschatology.

In the last century, Emily Dickinson wrote:

> Safe in their Alabaster Chambers—
> Untouched by Morning—
> And untouched by Noon—
> Lie the meek members of the Resurrection—
> Rafter of Satin—and Roof of Stone![3]

Orthodoxy holds that there is an intermediate state—that the members of the resurrection are in a state of waiting—whether that be a state of simple anticipation or purgation. The more evangelical attitude is that the faithful departed are immediately in a state of joy and felicity. As for our bodies, whether immediately or later, all agree that we will be clothed with a new creation, a resurrection body that differs from this one, in that it is imperishable. In any event, the death of those who follow Christ is ultimately cause for joy.

But wait a minute. In all of this focus on future bliss, we might smell a rat. Haven't we heard something before about pie-in-the-sky? Hasn't this been used to justify the misuse and drudgery of many, many lives? We live in a culture and a world obsessed with death, capable of global suicide while constantly denying death's reality. Isn't this more justification of our greed and privilege, with the assumption that equity and justice will come about later on when there will be no material or social limitations? Isn't this just more of the same? To this Jesus responds, "I came that they may have life, and have it abundantly" (John 10:10)—beginning now.

Jesus did not die on the cross so that our lives on earth would be simply a preamble to our joy in heaven. Rather, Jesus came to teach us how to live on the earth so that we might realize its wonder, so that we might learn to love now.

In Thornton Wilder's play *Our Town*, Emily Webb has an opportunity to return from the dead, to return to earth for just one day. She chooses her twelfth birthday. She goes back with the knowledge of what will happen and of her death. She begins the day with the poignant awareness that we the living have no idea how beautiful and precious and fleeting this life is. "Oh, Mama," she says under her breath, "just look at me one minute as though you really saw me. Mama, fourteen years have gone by. I'm dead. You're a grandmother, Mama. I married George Gibbs, Mama. Wally's dead, too. Mama, his appendix burst on a camping trip to North Conway. We felt just terrible about it, don't you remember? But just for a moment we're happy. Let's look at one another."

But they don't, and Emily cannot stay the whole day. She says she cannot do it: "It goes so fast. We don't have time to look at one another." She returns to the dead, looking back, exclaiming, "Oh, earth, you're too wonderful for anyone to realize you."[4]

In the Gospel of John, Jesus says, "I have said these things to you so that my joy may be in you, and that your joy may be complete" (15:11). The possibilities of awakening to full self-awareness and full human responsibility happen within our biological life span. It is here that we do or do not achieve the image of God for which we were created. And as liberation theology has helped to point out, our salvation begins here and now.

The medieval rabbis used to say that if we could only see, each person is preceded by legions of angels singing, "Make way for the image of God." And so each of us is meant to be the image of God, the Christ, and our destiny is to permeate the mysteries that challenge us. Now we are a bit like chickens trying to comprehend Einstein's theory of relativity. So, we approach the mystery of love at the heart of eternity with the tools on which we've come to rely: our data banks and computers, our firm belief in facts and rationality. And we see as through a glass darkly. Someday we shall see face to face. But this we know now: There is joy in the final denouement. It is a divine comedy and not a tragedy in the end. "Where, O death, is your victory? Where, O death, where is your sting?" (1 Cor. 15:55).

There is celebration, abundant life, and great joy at the heart of the universe. As Chesterton observed, "we sit . . . in a starry chamber of silence, while the laughter of the heavens is too loud for us to hear."[5]

Chapter Seventeen

Sharing Our Wounds

John 20:19-31   TRY TO IMAGINE THE LAST OF THE TWELVE disciples. He is an old man about to die. He tries to encourage the young churches but is anxious about the day when there will be no one left who has seen the Lord. This was how the church viewed the disciple John, son of Zebedee and Salome, and the one thought to have been the authority behind, if not the author of, the Johannine canon which includes the Gospel, the Epistles, and the Revelation to John. He was the last survivor, the last eyewitness, who included in his Gospel the last beatitude of Jesus, "Blessed are those who have not seen and yet have come to believe." It is clear he keenly felt the need for convinced and convincing witnesses. Thomas Carlyle once said that what every church needs is someone who knows God at more than secondhand.[1]

One significant and sometimes overlooked way in which we can know God at more than secondhand was revealed to us by our Lord. It is through the sharing of our wounds. Yes, wounds. There is a large Roman Catholic church in San Jose, California, called the Church of the Five Wounds, and the name refers to the five wounds Jesus received at the Crucifixion: two in his hands, two in his feet, and one in his side.

In the twentieth chapter of the Gospel of John, we have a graphic story of those wounds. Jesus miraculously appears to a group of frightened disciples. Imagine their astonishment. They must have been feeling so discouraged, having let down their Lord in so many ways, and at the same time feeling let down by him who had died in such an ignominious way.

Then, despite the closed door, he is suddenly there in their midst, bidding them peace. Jesus opens his hands and shows them his side, and they rejoice for then they recognize the Lord. They know him by his wounds, they recognize him by those marks, and Jesus seemed to know that those marks would reveal him to his disciples. In many ways, it is by our wounds that we recognize one another, although it may not seem so at first. Our character is in large part what we have made with the blows life has dealt us. So, in part we know one another by our wounds, and whether we are healed or remain broken is determined by what we have made of our injuries.

The Gospel tells us that Thomas is not with the disciples at this time, and he later questioned Jesus' appearance saying, "Unless I see the mark of the nails in his hands, and put my finger in the mark of the nails and my hand in his side, I will not believe." Thomas seemed to be the kind of person who liked facts and operated accordingly. Eight days later, Jesus appears to the disciples again and says to Thomas, "Put your finger here and see my hands. Reach out your hand and put it in my side. Do not doubt but believe." Jesus invites Thomas to know his wounds, even intimately, and in doing so, Thomas recognizes Jesus and says those convinced and convincing words, "My Lord and my God!"

Not long ago I heard a tragic but common story, that of an apparently successful man who had committed suicide. This man had told no one of his deep and abiding despair. He was unable to share his wounds, and no one had thought to reach in and share their own with him. Ultimately, he was consumed by his hurts rather than being healed. The sharing of our wounds enables us to be healed; it also helps others to heal when they know we have suffered likewise. To share wounds need not be morbid or self-indulgent. It can be the way that we bear one another's burdens and so facilitate healing. In fact, those most able to heal others know intimately of human suffering; Henri Nouwen calls them "wounded healers."

Jesus suffered. We ignore his humanity and our own at our own expense. Some Christian traditions emphasize the suffering of Christ, particularly the Latin cultures. American Protestantism and mainstream American culture do not. But we ignore it at our peril.

Jesus suffered. He suffered in the desert when he was tempted. He wept at the death of his friend. And finally he was humiliated, beaten, mocked, and physically tortured to death in the Crucifixion. He knows our sorrows and our wounds. He has been there. He knows the sorrow of love betrayed, of friendship lost. He knows of unjust people in high places, of the valuing of money over human life. He knows the hypocrites who posture as religious leaders and those who prefer possessions to the kingdom of God. He knows our sorrows; he has felt them. But we, as a nation and as a culture, seem to want to deny that we have ever suffered. We want to be rugged individualists, sleek successes with no wounds to show or to share.

Alan Jones, Dean of Grace Cathedral in San Francisco, tells of an ancient legend in which the devil tries to get into heaven by pretending to be the risen Christ. Disguised and decked out in light and splendor, he arrives at the gates of heaven with a band of demons dressed as angels of light. He shouts out the words of the psalm, "Lift up your heads, O gates! and be lifted up, O ancient doors! that the King of glory may come in." The angels in heaven are delighted and respond with the psalm's refrain, "Who is the King of glory?" Satan boldly opens his arms and says, "I am." But in doing so, he shows that there are no marks on his hands. The angels see that he is an impostor and the gates of heaven slam shut against him.[2]

If we are going to be real, authentic people, we will have wounds. We have felt things: love, joy, hurt, pain; and we have suffered if we have grown, for suffering and healing are part of human growth. Each of us is made in the image of God, and sometimes that image is hanging from a cross. In the child's book, *The Velveteen Rabbit*, the Skin Horse tells the Velveteen Rabbit the secret to becoming real, "It doesn't happen all at once. You become. It takes a long time. That's why it doesn't often happen to people who break easily or have sharp edges, or who have to be carefully kept. Generally, by the time you are Real, most of your hair has been loved off, and your eyes drop out and you get loose in the joints and very shabby. But these things don't matter at all, because once you are Real you can't be ugly, except to people who don't understand."[3]

Real people have wounds, and they share them with others in helping them to be healed, to find faith again. All of us can be wounded healers; or we can hide our wounds, try to present an unreal image to the world, and despair alone. Our wounds are the marks of our growth and change. When we share our wounds, we act in the faith that there is meaning in suffering and that God is acting in our history, individually and corporately. The message that the risen Christ brought to the disciples on Easter morning is that each body, wounds and all, is bound for glory. But each of us needs to get in shape for glory, to "practice resurrection,"[4] and part of practicing resurrection is sharing our wounds.

Remember that it was his wounds that enabled the disciples to know the risen Lord. Wounds can help us to find the Christ in others and in ourselves. When we share our wounds, when we trust that they have meaning, when we strive to be real, authentic people, when we practice resurrection, then we find that the Lord is with us—not a secondhand knowledge of God, but the living God of Easter.

Chapter Eighteen

Always Is Always Now

Come Holy Spirit.
Come as the wind and cleanse us.
Come as the fire and purge us.
Come as the dove and lift our hearts.
Convict, convert, consecrate us
that we may claim your Pentecostal gifts. Amen.

1 Corinthians 12:4-13

HAVE YOU EVER HAD A TIME when you felt lifted out of time, as if time itself had slowed or almost stopped, as if it had ceased to measure its minutes, or they had ceased to matter? The poet Philip Larkin wrote of such a moment with his beloved, saying:

> I take you now and always,
> for always is always now.[1]

Have you ever felt an eternal moment—that "always is always now"? Sometimes loving family times feel that way, or quiet evenings at home with a good book and a long twilight. Sometimes looking at a beloved face, a child asleep, an old friend can stop the clock. It has been my experience that such moments have to do with a sense of belonging to the universe, of the rightness of my existence, and the reality of love.

"Redeem the time," said T. S. Eliot, and on a beautiful spring day in this year of our Lord, as we sit in church, we may not see time as in need of redemption. Time may seem to be no problem. Yet if we pause and reflect on time, we realize that it is one of the great problems for philosophers in particular and human beings in general. We realize that the battle against time and the erosions time brings fill much of our daily lives. We note the signs of aging on ourselves, our loved ones. We see things deteriorate—our houses, cars, roads, resolutions, relationships. We struggle to maintain them, but things fall apart. Entropy seems the rule. We take security measures against time and transience, death and disease. As business mogul Malcolm Forbes said, "By the time we've made it, we've had it."[2]

And we live in history. If we read the daily newspapers, we see what a sorry cavalcade of life history is. There is war and rumor of war, crime and cruelty, disease and catastrophe, scandal and degeneration. Good news is infrequent and seldom on the front page. Our lives fit into this larger history and at times are absorbed by it.

"Redeem the time," the poet cries. "With what are we to change, redeem, convert the time?" we ask. To which we are answered: "The conversion of time by the Holy Ghost is . . . the grand activity of the Church."[3] And that brings us to the great anniversary of the birth of the Church when the Holy Spirit came to seize its ragtag membership with power and authority. I have no doubt but that the first Pentecost was a time out of time for those first Christians. They were so suffused with joy, purpose, and belonging to the universe that they were mistaken by some as drunk.

They had been promised the Holy Spirit (John 20:19-23) and Jesus had breathed on them, asking them to receive it. Still, the experience of the first Pentecost was unexpected. It was the Jewish Feast of Weeks, one of the three most important Jewish festivals, and it focused on thanksgiving for the harvest and the giving of the law. It came seven weeks after Passover, and so came to be known as Pentecost (a Greek word meaning "fiftieth") because it was celebrated fifty days after the Sabbath on which Passover began.

The disciples were gathered in Jerusalem, when suddenly there was a sound like a mighty wind and flames like tongues of fire appeared over each of them. Then they began to speak in many languages about the wonders of God. Jews from the far-flung regions of the Diaspora gathered around them and could suddenly hear what was being said in their individual languages, and they marveled at what was happening.

What was happening was that the Holy Spirit, the third person of the Trinity, God at work in the church and in the world, had entered the disciples. Now, this was not the first appearance of the Holy Spirit in history. It was the Holy Spirit who brooded over creation in the beginning of the world. It was the Holy Spirit who spoke through the prophets. It was the Holy Spirit by whom Jesus was conceived in Mary. And the Holy Spirit is still acting today in the church and in the process by which each of us is drawn closer and closer to God.

The Holy Spirit was there from the beginning. In Hebrew and Aramaic, Jesus' native language, the word is *ruach*, which means breath or wind, and it is feminine in gender. The Greek word *pneuma* also means wind and is neuter in gender. In English we have referred to the Holy Spirit as "he," but "she" may be more appropriate and would be historically correct. In any case, it is the Holy Spirit who redeems the time.

And she does this by dispensing gifts to us, making us the agents of redemption. In his First Letter to the Corinthians, Paul discusses nine manifestations, or ways in which the Spirit is made known among us. They are dispensed as generously as a mother is eager to give good things to her children.

These are the gifts that are given for the building up of the common good, and I would like for you to listen as I name them. I would like for you to listen for the one gift that calls out for you. I would ask you to take that gift; take it down off the shelf, out of the box, so to speak, and put it on. And as the Spirit is most generous, you are not limited to one. You may take as many as you like.

You are warranted to do this because Paul says elsewhere to put on the new nature of Christ. While we as a church are the mystical body of Christ, it is still a choice—this putting on of the Christ nature—and the choice is yours. The gifts are there for your taking. Take the one or more that you need, the ones that call your name. With them you can create eternal moments out of the march of time.

The first manifestation of the Spirit is wisdom, another name by which the Holy Spirit has been known. It is an ability to synthesize information and experience to the benefit of others. It is a mystery comprised of God, human conscience, and human experience. It often comes with age, but not necessarily.

Akin to it is the second gift, that of knowledge, the accumulation and distillation of information which enriches the church and the world. In the academic world, knowledge is the main commodity. It can solve many of the world's problems.

Third is faith, one of the three theological virtues, and that quality in his followers by which Jesus claimed most miracles were wrought. You recall that he often said, "Your faith has made you well." It is also the light by which the church is guided.

Fourth is the gift of healing, of caring for the well-being of the body, mind, and spirit of another. This vital gift, often demonstrated by our Lord in his ministry helps us understand why we call the Holy Spirit the Comforter.

Fifth is the gift of miraculous powers, of moving beyond our natural capacity. Such powers may be supernatural or within the natural order. This gift is demonstrated by those who survive and prevail against great odds and those who maintain their humanity when inhumanity is all around them. Nelson Mandela is an example who comes to mind.

Sixth is the capacity for prophecy, for seeing the hand and direction of God in history, not only in the future but in the present. The Holy Spirit has spoken through the prophets, and that voice is among us still, directing the church where it needs to go.

Seventh is the ability to distinguish between spirits, the gift of discernment. This is the gift of seeing into the heart of things—of people, movements, times. It is the ability to know the source behind words and actions, so that the church chooses well.

Eighth is the gift of speaking in tongues, the same gift that the disciples received on the first Pentecost. It is that which communicates to another in his or her own tongue, that which conveys the message of God's good news. It can be through language or through other media, such as the arts—music, dance, painting.

Ninth and last is the interpretation of tongues; that which increases and enhances communication, broadening the message and the number of those who understand. Interpretation is the means by which more can hear the good news.

Which gift called your name? Which ones asked for you? Take them today. Put them on and trust that a flame is being kindled inside you now. These are your tools for redeeming the time. With them you can wrest time from its relentless movement toward decay and death, and claim it for eternity. That is the grand activity of the church, and you are the church. Take these gifts and use them. They are yours now, and always, "for always is always now."

Chapter Nineteen

The Fullness of the One Who Fills All in All

Ephesians 1:15-23 | A CRISIS OF FAITH CAN COME UPON A Christian unprepared. It is almost as if we wake up one morning and all is changed. Suffering an injustice or a major loss can create doubt. Even weariness or depression can make us feel we have fallen from grace, lost connection with God, been abandoned.

In my own life such a time occurred while I was in seminary, studying for a year in Aberystwyth, Wales. Suddenly, without warning, I found myself feeling cut off from God, mouthing prayers that seemed to echo in my own head and feeling adrift, lost, and afraid. It seemed an interminable time of silence and loss. In later years I would come to understand this time as a desert experience, a dark night of the soul, a transition in my own faith development. But, at the time, it was an acutely painful separation, and my only sure companion was the unrelenting silence of God.

Have you ever wondered if the disciples and followers of Jesus might have felt such a loss at the time of the Ascension? Perhaps you remember seeing depictions of the Ascension event, either in art books or in older churches. The followers are standing on a mountain looking up, and from the top of the picture we see two feet hanging from the heavens. Do you wonder if a few of the followers didn't feel desperate, didn't want to grab onto those feet, as a child might catch an escaping balloon, and beg Jesus to stay just a while longer, or at least take them with him?

This departure marks the time in the life of the first Christians when the risen Lord would return to God and they would experience Christ's presence in a different way. The event is chronicled several places in Scripture, with Luke's account in the Acts of the Apostles being the most complete and least questioned. Jesus' ascension concludes forty days of being with the apostles since the Resurrection. He promises that they will receive the power of the Holy Spirit, and then he is lifted up, and a cloud takes him out of sight. After he is gone, two men in white robes appear, proclaiming that Jesus will return in the same manner by which he left.

Anytime someone we love goes away, whether they leave the area permanently or they die, we experience loss. There are stages of mourning that we pass through in coming to terms with every loss. One of the first stages is denial, and shock comes fast on its heels. Then come the many faces of grief: There is acute pain and longing, anger over our powerlessness to change the situation, guilt over what we might have done better. There are emotional swings—fear fluttering in our breast, lapses in thinking. We may miss appointments, become easily confused, feel overwhelmed. Engulfing these symptoms is a pervasive sadness.

Slowly we progress. With love and support and the tincture of time, we gradually achieve an acceptance of our loss, and healing takes place. But with every loss, we are changed. How we are changed will depend on how we come to understand the loss over time. When we think of Jesus' leave-taking, we may wonder how the disciples came to understand his words, "I am with you always, to the end of the age" (Matt. 28:20). They are comforting but bewildering words. Jesus says he will be with us, through it all, to the end of time.

Paul's Letter to the Ephesians offers us a deep and rich understanding of those words. Paul speaks of the power of God that works for those who believe, enlightening them and giving them hope. He goes on to say that "God put this power to work in Christ when he raised him from the dead and seated him at his right hand in the heavenly places. . . . And he put all things under his feet and has made him the head over all things for the church, which is his body, the fullness of him who fills all in all."

In this passage, Paul conceives of Jesus as growing larger and more comprehensive. Later in this same epistle he describes Jesus as the one "who ascended far above all the heavens, so that he might fill all things" (Eph. 4:10). We are being asked to stretch and expand our understanding of Christ, moving from the Jesus of history—a first-century Jew with a human body and life that began, as all of us did, from a single cell—to the Christ of faith—a cosmic reality that incorporates all of us into his universal body now. We are urged to think in a most comprehensive and revolutionary way, to allow the old wineskins of our understanding to burst and to let the heady new wine take us into uncharted and dizzying new places.

In Salvador Dali's painting *The Last Supper,* Jesus is seated with his disciples, and on the table is the broken bread that he has consecrated to be his body. At first glance, the painting looks like many depictions we have seen of the Last Supper. But a closer look shows that an amazing thing is happening in the picture. The body of Jesus, the body of Christ, is becoming transparent, and we can see through his chest and arms to the sea and boats behind him. Through him we are seeing the world, but seeing it differently—we are seeing Christ becoming the world.

The twentieth-century paleontologist and theologian Teilhard de Chardin wrote, "Since first you said, Lord, 'This is my body,' not only the bread of the altar, but (to a certain extent) everything in the universe that nourishes the soul for the life of Spirit and Grace, has become *yours,* become *divine*—it is divinized, divinizing, and divinizable. Every presence makes me feel that you are near me; every contact is the touch of your hand."[1]

In the same vein, J. B. Phillips, who wrote one modern translation of the New Testament, coined the phrase "your God is too small" and wrote a book by that title. We might better understand the Ascension as the completion of a mystery that challenges and amazes us. In his Letter to the Ephesians, Paul prays "that . . . the eyes of your heart [may be] enlightened." Such an understanding of Christ becoming the cosmos will strike each of us as no less than revelation. In his ascension, Jesus has transcended space and time, entering all space and all time, and visible in all the forces of the universe if we but have eyes to see.

I began by telling you about a crisis of faith that I underwent, but I didn't tell you how it was resolved. Over time, the silence of God that had felt so cold and distancing began to change. I began to sense a presence in its depths and gradually found comfort in it. Eventually, I found my theology changing, and I realized that the silence of God was paradoxically the way God had spoken to me. God's silence enabled me to hear God in other voices as well as the silence. I found that God was still with me, teaching me a new and deeper intimacy, and seeking me as actively as I had been seeking God.

In every loss there are seeds of change. Haven't you found that your losses are often the means by which you grow? I think it is the same for an individual, as for a congregation, and a community. In retrospect don't you sometimes find that what initially looked like a great loss came to give you a great gift? I know that is so with the departure of Jesus: the person of one human being who taught, loved, healed, challenged, and transformed people in first-century Palestine has been transformed by the power of God to fill all of creation with the presence of sacrificing love.

Jesus promised that he would be with us always, even to the end of time. Let us seek to find him in the world around us, especially when we feel lost and alone. Let us trust that there is presence there, seeking us, even when we don't perceive it. And let us remember that we are all Christ's body, and that through Christ and with Christ and in Christ we participate in "the fullness of him who fills all in all."

Chapter Twenty

Salt and Light

Matthew 5:13-16

I DON'T REMEMBER MY BAPTISM, BUT I HAVE a small, white, leather-bound King James Version of the Bible that my paternal grandmother gave me for the occasion. It is now tattered and worn, but my name is still embossed in gold on the cover, and inside, in a childish scrawl, is what was probably my first attempt at theology. I had written a question and answer that to this day probably best summarizes why I am a follower of Christ. I wrote, "Why do I love him?" and below that I answered, "Because he is so kind." Because he is so kind. What is kindness ultimately but the treatment we receive from one like us? One who understands us and is on our side: our kin, our kind. Kin, kindred, and kindness all share common roots of language, and those qualities, which we think of as kind—courtesy, empathy, benevolence, gentleness, and generosity—reflect an evolved understanding of what it means to be one of our kind.

Let me tell you a story about kindness. Years ago on a night flight from New York to the West Coast, I went up to the lounge of the huge 747 to get a soft drink. An older woman with an Eastern European accent asked if she could join me. We began talking, and she asked about my family and then began to tell me about hers. She had a son teaching in Boston and a daughter living on a kibbutz in Israel. I assumed my companion was Jewish; and when I made a remark to that effect, she explained that she was a Christian but had raised her daughter as a Jew. When I asked why, she told me this story:

When the Nazis came to her village in Poland to round up the Jews for removal to the camps, no one really knew what was happening; but everyone knew it was something dreadful. The smell of death was in the air. This woman was doing her weekly shopping near the train station the day the Nazis arrived. Gestapo officers were pushing the Jewish villagers onto the trains, and one was pushing a woman who had a little girl with her. He turned to the Jewish woman and, pointing to her daughter, roughly asked, "Is this your child?"

The woman stopped, looked straight at my companion, and said, "No, she's hers."

"And so you took her daughter?" I asked.

"Yes," she nodded. "What would you have done?"

It is sometimes hard to believe that the Holy One from all eternity, who set in motion the sun and the stars, could take our human nature and become our kind. Yet that is our Christian understanding expressed in the doctrine of the Incarnation. This God who embodied kindness invites us to partake of that kinship and kindness in ever-deepening ways. By kindness, I do not mean niceness or sweetness; rather, I mean behavior that comes from the conviction that we belong to one another. Kindness is when "those folks" become "our folks."

It has often struck me as strange that our faith tradition is so trivialized, sentimentalized, and seriously misunderstood in our secular culture. I remember my amazement upon reading, for the first time, the Gospels in their entirety. I was in my twenties, a child of the turbulent 1960s. The Gospels were astonishing, much more revolutionary than anything else I'd encountered and yet, mysteriously, had been preserved in a society that paid homage to them, apparently without reading them. Religion is respected by the average American but deemed a rather strange, unnatural place, vague and obscure and lacking the reality of other areas of life. Some even suspect Christianity of being delusional. And so our secular culture dismisses or trivializes our faith while reading the Sunday horoscopes or test-driving an automobile named Infiniti. As a culture, we are, in Alan Jones' words, "spiritually hungry and religiously illiterate."[1]

Contrary to our culture's view of religion, the Gospel makes extravagant claims about the significance and importance of the believer's life in the world. Jesus tells his friends and followers that we are "the salt of the earth" and "the light of the world." He then urges us to retain and display those qualities to others that they, too, might come to know God.

When we act out of kindness, it makes an impression; for all of us, at times, feel excluded from the human family, and it is then that we most need kinship. A dear friend told me that during her first year of college she went through a particularly difficult time. A number of failures and disappointments converged until she felt she was cut off, adrift, and spiraling down into a dark, lost place from which she might never return. She recalled that another woman from an adjacent dormitory—a sophomore from her hometown, a person she knew, but not a close friend—stopped by her room and sensed that something was terribly wrong. She sat by my friend and spoke soothingly and evenly of common experiences of their town, of mutual friends, of shared events. She stayed a long time, brought hot tea, kept remembering. My friend gradually felt herself emerging and being located and anchored back into the present world. She wondered in later years if the other woman ever knew how important her kindness, her kinship, had been.

To be the salt of the earth and the light of the world is sometimes simply showing that we belong to one another. The deep disease of us all is the denial of this fundamental law of our being. We seek to possess in either spiritual or material things what we can have only in the community of giving and receiving.

Let's look for a moment at the assembly to which Jesus spoke. There were fundamentally two different kinds of people there. There were people not at peace with this world: hungry, poor, oppressed people eagerly hoping for deliverance. These were people who wanted change, justice, freedom from material and spiritual want. And alongside them on that mountainside was another group of people. They were comfortable in their lives, enjoying security, power, and prestige. They were well-adjusted and at home in the ways of the world. They did not want things to change.

The situation I've just described in Galilee is still our situation today. And the main difference between the two groups is not simply economic, that one is rich and one is poor. The main difference is that the first group is open to the transforming work of God and lives both in this world and in the reign of God that is to come. The second group lives only in this world.

"You are the salt of the earth. . . . You are the light of the world." Salt and light. What exactly does Jesus mean by these strange and compelling terms? First, let's look at salt. Salt is a white or clear solid compound, an ordinary commodity, but an extremely precious one because without it we cannot live. It is also what makes many foods taste good and is a basic preservative, allowing us to eat through the frozen winter, the scorching summer. It has cleansing and even healing properties but can sting if it touches a wound.

No doubt Jesus' hearers wondered at their own preservative and purifying properties. Pure sodium chloride does not deteriorate; but people do, morals do, our best laid plans do. Jesus knew that people, unlike salt, could lose their savor and their saltiness and that they would be rendered useless if they did.

Salt enables and enhances life, making what is good even better. With a little poetic license we can say that this simple, basic necessity of life speaks of and for the earth, adding zest and humor, challenging pomposity while maintaining fundamental values. When we say someone is "the salt of the earth," that's what we mean.

Jesus also says, "You are the light of the world." The rabbis of that period used to refer to God as the light of the world, and Jesus used the phrase to describe the listening multitude on the mountainside. The phrase "the light of the world" is only found one other place in Scripture, and that is in the Gospel of John. There Jesus says, "I am the light of the world" (8:12). So Jesus describes both himself and his disciples with the same metaphor. We are clearly invited to share in his purpose, to bring about the reign of the God of love. And we are named and called to be bright beacons of that reign.

This does not confer superiority on the followers of Christ; rather, it gives us a great responsibility and a high calling. We are entrusted with the flame, as it were, but it is only ours insofar as we remain in touch with the source of the fire. Pride, or thinking we own the light, can put it out; but if it shines genuinely, it cannot be concealed.

These words no doubt seemed high and magnificent for the ordinary people who were following Jesus. It was comparable to saying, "You sit on the right hand of God." People, then as now, questioned their self-worth. But what if we are, indeed, the light of the world? When in doubt, why don't we believe our Lord's words and take them as true?

All children are at first afraid of the dark and perhaps we still are—not afraid of the shadows at the top of the stairs but of the darkness of evil, of hatred, of nothingness. And yet Jesus calls us to stand against that, and as Christians, we must.

In 1555 two English bishops, Hugh Latimer and Nicholas Ridley, were burned at the stake for attempting to reform the English church. Bishop Latimer was an old man who wore his shroud to the execution. As the executioners kindled the fagots, he turned to Bishop Ridley, who was dressed in the vestments of his office, and said, "Be of good comfort, Master Ridley, and play the man; we shall this day light such a candle by God's grace in England as (I trust) shall never be put out."[2]

Could it be that we are to be the lights when the other lights go out? When other friends and lovers fail, when alcohol and drugs have shown their dead ends, when the world's promises have let us down, when evil is mobilized and death at the door—perhaps then we are to summon our light and let it shine.

Once in New York I took the wrong subway train and found myself in a very dangerous neighborhood. I asked the subway ticket agent in her barred office if I could catch a cab at the top of the stairs. She said she wouldn't go up those stairs if she were I; rather, she suggested that I take the next train to the end of the line and then return to my proper destination. I was suddenly frightened. All around me were men in overcoats, looking ominous. With the exception of the ticket agent, I was the only woman. I grew more and more afraid and realized I was visibly shaking. I knew enough about urban living to know that I should not appear vulnerable, so I put my head down to cover the tears that were welling in my eyes. Slowly, I became aware that the whole group was gathering, and the men were closing in on me. I prayed that the train would come when one of them spoke quietly and said, "What's the matter, dear?"

I looked up and, without thinking, said, "I'm scared."

He responded, "Ain't none of us going to let anybody hurt you. Don't you worry, now. We're here."

The source of my immediate fear had suddenly become one of comfort. Seldom have I felt so chastened and warmed at once.

All of us are afraid of the dark, and yet each of us is called to be the light; not light-bringers as bearers of wisdom and knowledge (although that may be a by-product), but simply by illuminating the larger truth that we belong to one another. We see it in a stranger who raised a doomed woman's child as she would have wished; in a sister-student who used the tools she had to rescue a friend; in the bright and searing flames of the martyrdom of bishops; and in an unknown man in a subway who cared for a stranger, taking her in and allowing the light of Christ to shine in that underground gloom long enough to teach her something of the kingdom of heaven.

Salt and light. Emily Dickinson once said, "It's such a common glory."[3] It is a common glory. The humble and the splendid. Salt and light. That's what Jesus says we are and continues to call us to be.

Notes

Introduction

1. Romano Guardini, quoted in Anne Sexton, *All My Pretty Ones* (Boston: Houghton Mifflin, 1961), 17.
2. Iranaeus, quoted in Bjarne Skard, *The Incarnation: A Study in the Christology of the Ecumenical Creeds*, trans. Herman E. Jorgensen (Minneapolis: Augsburg Publishing House, 1960), 30.
3. Thomas F. Torrance, ed., *The Incarnation: Ecumenical Studies in the Nicene-Constantinopolitan Creed A.D. 361* (Edinburgh: The Handsel Press, Ltd., 1981), XVI.
4. Shirley C. Guthrie, *Christian Doctrine* (Louisville: Westminster/John Knox Press, 1994), 54.
5. Rosemary Haughton, *The Passionate God* (New York: Paulist Press, 1981), 9.
6. Mary Oliver, "West Wind 3," *West Wind* (Boston: Houghton Mifflin, 1997), 47.

Chapter 1. "I Am"

1. John Sanford, *Mystical Christianity: A Psychological Commentary on the Gospel of John* (New York: Crossroad, 1994), 107.
2. Ibid., 117.
3. Christopher Smart, "Christmas Day," *The Oxford Book of Christmas Poems*, ed. Michael Harrison and Christopher Stuart-Clark (Oxford: Oxford University Press, 1983).

Chapter 2. "Learn from Me"

1. Robert Coles, *The Story of Ruby Bridges* (New York: Scholastic, 1995).
2. Penelope Duckworth, "Laude," *Yankee*, May 1992, 128.
3. Italics mine.
4. William Temple, *Daily Readings from William Temple*, comp. Hugh C. Warner, ed. William Wand (Nashville: Abingdon Press, 1965), 183.
5. Frederick Buechner, *Wishful Thinking: A Theological ABC* (New York: Harper & Row, 1973), 80-81.

Chapter 3. "Will You Carry Me?"

1. Madeleine L'Engle, *The Irrational Season* (San Francisco: Harper & Row, 1977), 27.
2. T. Pestel, "Behold the Great Creator Makes," *Hymns for All Seasons Sung by the Choir of St. John's College, Cambridge* (London: Decca Record Co., n.d.).

3. Frederick Buechner, *The Faces of Jesus* (New York: Stern/Harper & Row, 1989), 27.

4. Bill Kellermann, "O Holy Nightmare: Incarnation and Apocalypse," *Sojourners*, December 1985, 36. (I am indebted to Bill Kellermann for several ideas expressed in this sermon.)

5. Antonio Machado, *Times Alone: Selected Poems of Antonio Machado*, trans. Robert Bly (Middletown: Wesleyan, 1983), 51.

Chapter 4. Gifts and Revelations

1. Lewis Hyde, *The Gift* (New York: Vintage Books, 1979), 3-4.

2. Penelope Duckworth, "Epiphany," *The Episcopalian/Professional Pages*, January 1989, 1.

3. Theodore Roethke, "The Lost Son," *The Collected Poems of Theodore Roethke* (Garden City: Doubleday, 1966), 58.

Chapter 5. The Incarnate Word

1. Hans Urs von Balthasar, *A Theological Anthropology* (New York: Sheed & Ward, 1967), 239.

2. Lancelot Andrewes, *Seventeen Sermons on the Nativity* (London: Griffith, Farran, Okenden, & Welsh, *The Ancient and Modern Library of Theological Literature*, n.d.), 88. (I am indebted to Rabbi Patricia Karlin-Neumann, Associate Dean for Religious Life at Stanford University, for clarification of the Hebrew.)

3. Jacob Needleman, *The Little Book of Love* (New York: Doubleday, 1996), 43.

4. Emily Dickinson, *The Complete Poems of Emily Dickinson*, ed. Thomas H. Johnson (Boston: Little, Brown, 1960), 534-35.

Chapter 6. Requisite Virtue

1. C. S. Lewis, *The Four Loves* (New York: Harcourt Brace Jovanovich, 1960).

2. Oscar Wilde, quoted in *The Choice Is Always Ours*, ed. Dorothy Berkley Phillips, Elizabeth Boyden Howes, and Lucille M. Nixon (New York: Family Library, 1975), 137.

3. Henry James, quoted in Frederick Buechner, "Be Holy," *Best Sermons 2*, ed. James W. Cox (San Francisco: Harper & Row, 1989), 205-206.

4. Dante, *The Divine Comedy, Il Purgatorio*, trans. John D. Sinclair (New York: Oxford University Press, 1939), 131-69.

5. Frederick Buechner, *Wishful Thinking: A Theological ABC* (New York: Harper & Row, 1973), 40.

6. Attributed to Francis of Assisi, from a poster by Sr. Corita Kent, circa 1970.

Chapter 8. The Lord Is My Shepherd

1. William Temple, *Daily Readings from William Temple*, comp. Hugh C. Warner, ed. William Wand (Nashville: Abingdon Press, 1965), 183.

2. Flora Wuellner, *Prayer, Stress and Our Inner Wounds* (Nashville: The Upper Room, 1985), 11.

3. C. S. Lewis, *Miracles* (New York: Macmillan, 1952), 111.

4. Oscar Wilde, "E Tenebris," *Chapters into Verse*, vol. II, ed. Robert Atwan and Laurance Wieder (Oxford: Oxford University Press, 1993), 110.

Chapter 9. "Lord, . . . How Often . . . ?"

1. William Blake, *A Selection of Poems and Letters*, ed. J. Bronowski (New York: Penguin Books, 1958), 34.
2. The *San Jose Mercury News*, Sept. 9, 1990, B1.

Chapter 10. The Abomination of Desolation

1. Amos Wilder, *Jesus' Parables and the War of Myths* (London: SPCK, 1982), 25.
2. Ibid., 153.
3. Ibid., 25.
4. *The Book of Common Prayer* (New York: Oxford University Press, 1979), 861-62.

Chapter 11. Creativity

1. Annie Dillard, *Pilgrim at Tinker Creek* (New York: Harper's Magazine Press, 1974), 112.
2. James Weldon Johnson, "Creation," *God's Trombones* (New York: Viking Press, 1927).
3. Rollo May, *The Courage to Create* (New York: W. W. Norton, 1975), 139-40.
4. Duke Ellington, quoted in Julia Cameron, *The Artist's Way: A Spiritual Path to Higher Creativity* (New York: G. P. Putnam's Sons, 1992), 62.
5. Mary Daly, quoted in Ibid., xiii.
6. Thomas Traherne, "You never enjoy the world aright," *The English Spirit: The Little Gidding Anthology of English Spirituality* (Nashville: Abingdon Press, 1987), 121. (Please note that I made slight changes to the text to bring it toward contemporary usage.)

Chapter 12. "Yes, Lord, Yet . . . "

1. Countee Cullen, "Incident," *On These I Stand* (San Francisco: Harper & Row, 1947).
2. C. S. Lewis, *They Stand Together: The Letters of C. S. Lewis to Arthur Greeves (1914-1963)*, ed. Walter Hooper (The Estate of C. S. Lewis, 1979).
3. Mark 7:29 (italics mine).
4. Edwin Markham, *The Shoes of Happiness* (Garden City: Doubleday, Page & Co., 1915), 1.
5. Matthew 22:37 (italics mine).

Chapter 13. The Body of Christ

1. Leo Baeck, *Judaism and Christianity* (Philadelphia: The Jewish Publication Society of America, 1958), 31.
2. Robert McAfee Brown, *Unexpected News: Reading the Gospel with Third World Eyes* (Philadelphia: The Westminster Press, 1984), 132-33.
3. Robert McAfee Brown, *Liberation Theology* (Louisville: John Knox Press, 1993), 67.
4. Robert McAfee Brown, *Unexpected News*, 125.
5. Jim Forest, Making Friends of Enemies (New York: Crossroad Books, 1988).
6. Teresa of Avila, quoted in Rueben P. Job and Norman Shawchuck, *A Guide to Prayer for Ministers and Other Servants* (Nashville: The Upper Room, 1983), 22-23.

Chapter 15. God Forsaken

1. C. S. Lewis, *The Efficacy of Prayer* (Cincinnati: Forward Movement Publications, 1958).
2. John Saward, *The Mysteries of March: Hans Urs von Balthasar on the Incarnation and Easter* (Washington, D.C.: The Catholic University of America Press, 1990), 44.
3. Ibid., 47.
4. Rosemary Haughton, *The Passionate God* (New York: Paulist Press, 1981), 7.
5. Tertullian, "De Carne Christi," V, trans. Dr. Holmes, *Ante-Nicene Fathers*, vol. 3, ed. Alexander Roberts and James Donaldson (Grand Rapids: Wm. B. Eerdmans, 1973), 525. (I am indebted to Dean Robert Gregg of Stanford Memorial Church for helping me locate this quotation.)
6. George Herbert, "The Agony," *The Country Parson, The Temple*, ed. John N. Wall, Jr. (New York: Paulist Press, 1981), 151.

Chapter 16. Disbelief for Joy

1. Oscar Cullmann, *Immortality of the Soul; or, Resurrection of the Dead: The Witness of the New Testament* (London: Epworth Press, 1958).
2. G. K. Chesterton, *Orthodoxy* (Garden City: Doubleday, 1959), 160.
3. Emily Dickinson, *The Complete Poems of Emily Dickinson*, ed. Thomas H. Johnson (Boston: Little, Brown, 1960), 100.
4. Thornton Wilder, *Our Town* (New York: Coward McCann, Inc., 1938), 123ff.
5. G. K. Chesterton, *Orthodoxy*, 160.

Chapter 17. Sharing Our Wounds

1. Thomas Carlyle, quoted in *The Interpreter's Bible*, vol. 8 (Nashville: Abingdon Press, 1952), 800.
2. Alan Jones, *Passion for Pilgrimage* (San Francisco: Harper & Row, 1989), 150.
3. Margery Williams, *The Velveteen Rabbit* (New York: Derrydale Books, 1986), 14-15.
4. Wendell Berry, "Manifesto: The Mad Farmer Liberation Front," *Collected Poems: 1957-1982* (San Francisco: North Point Press, 1985), 151-52.

Chapter 18. Always Is Always Now

1. Philip Larkin, "It is for now or for always," *Collected Poems* (New York: Noonday Press, 1988), 296.
2. Malcolm Forbes, quoted in *Expect the Worst (You Won't Be Disappointed)*, ed. Eric Marcus (San Francisco: Harper, 1992), 101.
3. Charles Williams, *The Descent of the Dove* (Grand Rapids: Wm. B. Eerdmans, 1939), 15.

Chapter 19. The Fullness of the One Who Fills All in All

1. Teilhard de Chardin, "Le Milieu Mystique" (1917), Eng. trans. in *Writings in Time of War*, 146. Quoted in Robert Hale, O.S.B. Cam., *Christ and the Universe* (Chicago: Franciscan Herald Press, 1972), 24.

Chapter 20. Salt and Light

1. Alan Jones, "A Community of Communities: A Vision of Complete Unity in Unimaginable Diversity," *Grace Cathedral Annual Report*, January 14, 1990 (San Francisco: 1990), 11.
2. *The Proper for the Lesser Feasts and Fasts* (New York: The Church Hymnal Corporation, 1980), 346.
3. Emily Dickinson, *The Complete Poems of Emily Dickinson*, ed. Thomas H. Johnson (Boston: Little, Brown, 1960), 191.